AGAINST THE CHURCH

AGAINST THE CHURCH

Douglas Wilson

canonpress
Moscow, Idaho

Douglas Wilson, *Against the Church*
Copyright ©2013 by Douglas Wilson

Published by Canon Press
P. O. Box 8729, Moscow, Idaho 83843
800-488-2034 | www.canonpress.com

Cover design by David Dalbey
Cover and interior illustrations by Forrest Dickison
Interior design by Valerie Anne Bost
Printed in the United States of America

Unless otherwise indicated, all Scripture quotations are from the King James Version. Scripture quotations marked "NKJV" are from the New King James Version®. Copyright ©1982 by Thomas Nelson, Inc. Used by permission. All rights reserved.

Library of Congress Cataloging-in-Publication Data

Wilson, Douglas, 1953–
  Against the church / Douglas Wilson.
  pages cm
  ISBN 978-1-59128-141-2
  1. Church I. Title.
BV600.3.W565   2013
262—dc23

                                        2013023906

14 15 16 17 18 19 20   10 9 8 7 6 5 4 3

This book is for my friends at The Calvinist International. Steven and Peter, may you continue to stand for the church by standing against so much within the church.

CONTENTS

INTRODUCTION

THIS BOOK HAS FOUR SECTIONS. The first lays out the case against the church, both generally and in some particulars. After having made all sorts of people angry, the second section seeks to address certain background assumptions that go into these discussions—philosophical assumptions about human nature, dualism, and lots of other cool stuff. The third section is "The Father Principle," in which I discuss the source of life in the heart, the family, the church, and the world. The conclusion of the matter is where I seek to bring everything full circle, and lay out the case for the church. But if you look carefully, you will see that it is only possible to be for the church in this effectual way if you begin by mastering the case against the church.

When Peter Leithart wrote his book *Against Christianity*, he was addressing the very real problem of abstract theological idolatries. The modern man, ever since Descartes, has liked making idols out of intellectual abstractions. Leithart's fine book was a pointed stick jabbed into one eye of that great idol Religiosity, while this particular stick of mine, suitably sharpened by the editors, is intended for the other eye. While abstractions make fine idols, it would be a grave mistake to think that modern men are somehow immune from the age-old pitfalls presented by various *concrete* idolatries. We like candles and graven images almost as much as anybody.

Another wonderful blast against the abstract idolatries is Herbert Schlossberg's *Idols for Destruction*. There the idols of humanity, and power, and history are carefully dissected. I commend these works to everyone who will listen to me. But we have to be careful not to overestimate ourselves. The fact that we have mastered the art of identifying idols that we have forged in our minds and hearts does not mean at all that we have repented of forging them out of metals we dug from the ground.

So this is not an esoteric head trip. The issues addressed in this book are addressed over and over again throughout Scripture. One advantage I had in writing about such concrete idolatries is that, since Scripture antedates Descartes, I had a wealth of passages to resort to, passages that do not require a learned cultural translation before we make our applications.

When the Lord gave a vision of destruction to his prophet Ezekiel, a man with an ink horn marked all those who lamented over Judah's grievous idolatries. But to the other destroying angels, the Lord gave this disconcerting word:

"Slay utterly old and young, both maids, and little children, and women: but come not near any man upon whom is the mark; and begin at my sanctuary. Then they began at the ancient men which were before the house. And he said unto them, Defile the house, and fill the courts with the slain: go ye forth. And they went forth, and slew in the city" (Ezek. 9:6–7).

God often does not show sufficient respect to our holy things. And, we want to insist, they are only our holy things because we got them from *Him*. But these things—baptism and the Lord's Supper, and the principles of liturgy, and doctrine— were not given to us without accompanying instructions and cautions. God did not give us His Word as an invitation to start playing "pick and choose."

So it is no sacrilege to be "against the church." God is the ultimate iconoclast, and God told His angels to begin at His sanctuary, and He told them to get in there and defile it. That He had a higher purpose in mind can be seen elsewhere in the book of the prophet. And that I have a higher purpose can be seen in the latter half of this book.

PART ONE

AGAINST THE CHURCH

THE BRIDE OF CHRIST IS A HOT MESS

I AM SOMETIMES ASKED why I focus on the new birth so much. The question can be asked and answered on many different levels, but the foundational answer is that our condition is desperate. Like the Laodiceans (Rev. 3:18), we need to buy refined gold from Jesus, white garments to cover our shame, and eye salve so that we might come to see that we can't see anything.

We have all sorts of distractions to help persuade us that our condition is not in fact desperate, but those distractions always amount to some sort of Hezekiah-like "peace and safety in my time." We tend to measure how the culture is doing by how *we* are doing at the moment, which simply means that we are sentinels who can be bribed and bought off. A rising star who is finally breaking into the conference circuit, for example, and who thinks everything swell for that reason, is like a punter being put in as quarterback late in the fourth quarter, with the score something like 78 to 3. He thinks of it as a personal promotion, for *he* is now on the field, instead of seeing himself as being the crowning folly of a general disintegration in the coach's career.

So we need to come to grips with the fact that in North America, the bride of Christ is a hot mess.

We live in a time when the charismatics need the Spirit, the Reformed need a reformation, and the evangelicals need to be born again. We do not need particular doctrines about the Spirit in the abstract. If we are given the Spirit of reformation, we will get all the doctrines we need. We will of course need doctrine that arises from the Scriptures in order to help us understand what the Spirit just did for us. But if the Spirit didn't actually do anything, then our systematic theologies are nothing but printed kits for organizing smoke. If the Spirit didn't do anything, then any religious frenzies, conducted under an unauthorized use of His auspices, have all the religious authority of a priest of Baal cutting himself with a knife at a Stones concert.

But if the Spirit is poured out in power, then we will have what future generations will call a great reformation and revival. If He is not poured out, then we are in a desperate way, regardless of what we might think about it. Our situation is critical. But, some ask, if He is not poured out, what should we do in the meantime? That is a reasonable question, and we do have to do *something*. But everything we do should be in the spirit of Elijah arranging wood on the altar, waiting for the fire to fall, and recognizing the absolute need for the fire to fall. And when you get to the point of that showdown on Mount Carmel, there is no plan B.

In the meantime, we do not need for the bishop to process up the central aisle like the shiniest and baddest black crow in the gutter. We do not need another message from Doctrine Man with ten rivets in each subpoint. We do not need the worship leader to take us through yet one more orgasmic chord progression. We don't need a doctrine of responsible stewardship and sustainability that worries more about how many times we flush than how many babies we kill. We do not need any more cardboard cutout celebrity pastors, grinning at us, as smug as all dammit. In short, we don't need any more of what we currently have. A.W. Tozer once cuttingly observed that if revival means more of what we have now, we most emphatically do not need a revival.

In short, we need the Spirit to be poured out upon us. And when God is pleased to make this happen, the Spirit will do the work He always does, *which is that of making men new.* He will make them new in the middle of some metrosexual posedown in front of the mirror. He will make them new in the middle of some stupid sermon they are busy preaching, with puffs of dust arising every time a page is turned. He will make them new in the middle of an academic conference on feminist counternarratives. He will make them new in the middle of renting one more skeezefest on Netflix. He will make them new in the middle of their very last angry outburst against their wives. He will make them new while they are in the middle of yet another eggy Facebook post directed at what little faithfulness we have left. The Spirit will interrupt us, and He will make us new. That's what He does.

When the fire falls, everything worthwhile will be purified further, and will stand. Gold, silver, and gems will remain. But all the things we have made out of pine needles will go up in a sheet of flame—our celebrity conferences, our hair product youth pastors, our liturgical mummeries, our doctrinal gnat-strangling, and our arguments on the road—with Jesus just a couple yards in front of us—about who will be the greatest.

"I will praise the name of God with a song, and will magnify him with thanksgiving. This also shall please the Lord better than an ox or bullock that hath horns and hoofs . . . For God will save Zion, and will build the cities of Judah: that they may dwell there, and have it in possession. The seed also of his servants shall inherit it: and they that love his name shall dwell therein" (Ps. 69:30–31, 35–36).

So why do I write about this so much? Because we live in a valley of dry bones. This explains why a pastor would write a book against the church. This is why a preacher of sermons would write against sermons, why a practitioner of infant baptism would attack it, and given how many things are done in church, there is more where that came from. The explanation is that all who love the church *must* be against it. If you simply love and promote the church, one of the first things you will lose is the church. This is the very first lesson we need to learn in following Jesus, right? You have to lose things in order to save them. "For whosoever will save his life shall lose it; but whosoever shall lose his life for my sake and the gospel's, the same shall save it" (Mark 8:35). But you can't just lose things because of absentmindedness or carelessness. Jesus says that it has to be for *His* sake, and for the gospel's. If you lose the church for the sake of *Jesus* and for the sake of the *gospel*, you find at the end of the day that you have saved the church. In fact, it is the only way to save it.

AGAINST LITURGY

A CERTAIN MAN WAS TRAVELING TO MEMPHIS, and as he drove along the highway, he saw one of those big green road signs that said, "Memphis, 250 miles." This was not unusual, but what *was* unusual was the cluster of cars, tents, and Winnebagos around the base of the sign. Curious, he decided to stop.

As he walked up, a man stepped out of the closest Winnebago, and greeted him. "Greetings!"

"Hello," the traveler said. "What are you all doing here?"

"What does it look like?" the man said. "We're going to Memphis."

"How long have you been here?"

"Ten years or so. Or thereabouts."

"But that is not going to Memphis. You're just living right next to the sign to Memphis."

"Ah, but we know how many rivets are in the sign. And what kind of green paint it is. And how much paint they used. And the kind of concrete the posts are in. Do you know any of that stuff?"

"No," said the traveler, heading back to his car. "And I don't have time to learn. I have to be in Memphis by five."

The fact that liturgy is inescapable does not keep us from misusing it. In fact, it makes the misuse all the more likely. That old cynic Ambrose Bierce once defined ritualism as "A Dutch garden of God where He may walk in rectilinear freedom, keeping off the grass."[1] One of the early church fathers taught the principle *lex orandi, lex credenda*—the law of prayer is the law of faith. What this means is that our liturgies shape our faith; our liturgies are a confession of faith, and they are frequently a most *unexamined* statement of faith. We should be against anything that is shaping us unless we are being taught by Scripture at the same time. A telltale sign that we might be making this mistake is when we find ourselves parked in a Winnebago next to our liturgy, instead of using it to get somewhere else.

———

In all the sacred things we are against, we find the same error coming up again and again. Are we using the liturgy as mural or a window? Are we staring at it, or are we looking through it?

———

In the first chapter of Isaiah, we find all the necessary foundation stones for a true and robust evangelicalism. The Lord has called a people to Himself, having brought up children to Himself (Isa. 1:2). So they have a *formal* connection to Him, like good Episcopalians and Presbyterians, but those children have rebelled against Him. Their formal worship of God, their liturgy, had become corrupt (Isa. 1:11–15). This is not just some random thing they did, but rather it came about because they were a "seed of evildoers," they were "children that are corrupters" (Isa. 1:4). They did evil because they were evil. Their generation was all wrong, which meant there must be regeneration in order for it to be put right. The solution was

---

1   Ambrose Bierce, *The Devil's Dictionary* (Athens, GA: University of Georgia, 2000), 203.

to be converted. The answer is to have their sins, like scarlet, become as white as snow (Isa. 1:18). Their sins, which were as scarlet, included their scarlet liturgy.

When C.S. Lewis had been exasperated by a particular fallacy for quite long enough, he finally decided to name it. That is how we got *Bulverism*, the fallacy of dodging an opponent's argument by explaining first how he got to be so silly. In a similar vein, but not from so lofty a height, I have decided to name something that has been provoking me for some years now: the tendency that attempts to resist Gnosticism while simultaneously falling into something else very much like it.

Let's call it *knosticism*, shall we? The ancient error of gnosticism came from the Greek word for knowledge, *gnosis*. The Gnostics claimed to have an extra spiritual "something," a spark of heavenly knowledge, which trumped everything down here. It has come to mean a disparagement of the earthly and material, and a privileging of the rational, spiritual, or abstract. I have taken the English word knowledge and, using the latest advances in gene splicing, have translated this ancient tendency into its modern-English-speaking form—knosticism.

Many modern knostics have wanted to learn how to appreciate the arts of narrative. As far as that goes, nothing is wrong with it, but whether writing about novels, or movies, or stageplays, they have found "redemptive" or "death and resurrection" themes in all kinds of grimy stories. It turns out that *Dawn of the Dead* has resurrection themes. In other words, an abstract thing, the structure of the story, is mysteriously able to sanctify the actual content of the story. By means of this amazing magic trick, any amount of Tarantino sludge can be made edifying.

Now . . . three cheers for structure, but content matters. Content is determinative.

Given the title, I didn't expect to enjoy Mark Galli's book *Beyond Smells and Bells* quite as much as I did.[2] I found myself agreeing with virtually everything Galli wrote. He writes engagingly and with a great deal of practical wisdom. He is clearly one of the good guys. And yet we should object—*violently*—to an unstated assumption behind the book, an assumption that is quite common in our day. If the reader shares that knostic assumption, then this book will perpetuate confusion and do quite a bit of damage. If the reader hates that assumption as much as I do, throwing rocks at it every chance he gets, then he should profit from this book as much as I did. Shall I explain?

Galli is describing and defending a generic Western liturgy, and it is with that word *generic* that we get ourselves in trouble. In Appendix B, he has a helpful comparison of basic liturgies across denominational traditions—Roman, Lutheran, Anglican, Methodist, and Presbyterian. The point of the table is to show the astounding *structural* similarities between them. And, point taken—if the liturgy of Christ Church, where I minister, were to be included as a sixth column in that table, the similarities would continue to be just as obvious. In other words, I don't want to dispute this point at all, but I also want to maintain that this point is entirely beside the point.

I cannot tell, by examining these parallel liturgies, which tradition includes prayers to graven images. I cannot tell, by examining these liturgies, which ones allow the service to be led by a lesbian minister. In short, by looking at these liturgies, I cannot tell whether or not God receives them as "acceptable worship" or not. But whether or not God receives us in our offered worship is the central thing. In a line up of skeletons, I

---

2   Mark Galli, *Beyond Smells and Bells: The Wonder and Power of Christian Liturgy* (Brewster, MA: Paraclete Press, 2008).

cannot tell which one was the tattooed biker moll and which one was the Junior Miss princess.

The Bible teaches that the basic division in liturgical worship is not between high and low or between traditional and contemporary, but rather between *acceptable* and *unacceptable*. And the only thing that can make it acceptable is pure, unfeigned, evangelical faith in Jesus. Anything else is on its way to the Bad Place.

———

Right near the beginning of Scripture, we find the story of Cain's religious offering being rejected (Gen. 4:5). The people of Jeremiah's day are told that burnt offerings were not acceptable (Jer. 6:20)—they were just feigning heart religion (Jer. 3:10). Their hearts needed to be circumcised (Jer. 4:4). God refused to accept offerings from the hands of the Jews in Malachi's day (Mal. 1:10). We are called to worship God acceptably, with reverence and godly fear (Heb. 12:28). We ask God to remember all the offerings and to accept the burnt sacrifices (Ps. 20:3).

One of the reasons I emphasize regeneration so much is that this is the heart change that enables us to understand this critical point. Without the new birth, we are all of us sunk. When the worshipers are converted and regenerate, they fill out the worship service with acceptable content. And yes, I know this argument works just as well with those impudent organizers who think that the worship of God can be a junior high pep rally. Unconverted Protestants have figured out their own ways of offending God. Someone who is born again knows that God cannot be "worked." He knows that it is not our task to assemble before the Almighty in order to blow smoke at Him—whether or not thuribles are involved.

———

My friend Toby Sumpter, no enemy of robust liturgy, once wrote: "When people come to our church 'for the liturgy' I think I will begin asking how frequently they use porn, yell at their wife, or tell lies."[3] On a related note, Mark Galli, in his defense of liturgy, noted that "it should not surprise us that the liturgy is also one of the best places to hide from God."[4] It sure is.

When liturgists debate, they have a lot to talk about and many fields of study to cover—theology, history, aesthetics, and so on. I have certain decided convictions in all such debates and am happy to participate in them. But there is one thing needful as a prerequisite to everything else, and this one thing is necessary to keep all the subsequent debate from being entirely beside the point. You have to have Jesus.

If a man must be born again before he can see the kingdom of God, he must certainly be born again before he can see the realities of that kingdom in the liturgy. If you can't see the point, then you are not going to be able to see the point *anywhere.*

If the assembled people know and love God, then He receives their worship. If they do not, then He does not. If the assembled worshipers are spiritually dead, then all their liturgical accoutrements are just ornate carvings on the gravestones.

We should know that God is the great maker of icons. As the Creator of a world full of His image-bearers, He has made billions of them. If we know God, then we discern His body, we locate His image, and we will do so where *He* put it. If

---

3   Toby Sumpter, Twitter post, March 7, 2012, 1:47 p.m., http://twitter.com/TJSumpter.
4   Galli, *Beyond Smells and Bells,* 11.

we do not know God, then we will eventually find ourselves bowing down to pictures or statues that one of *us* made. Wisdom is as wisdom does, and people who pray to pictures don't have a liturgical clue.

And this is why it is necessary for us to confess that God is also the greatest iconoclast. As the Judge who governs a sinful world, He is the preeminent caster down of idols and images, especially those images or places or sacrifices or liturgies which He Himself commanded to be made in the first place. No one desecrates a holy place like YHWH. No one desecrates *His* holy places like YHWH. No one flings holy relics away in disgust like He does.

———

YHWH makes our ears to tingle (1 Sam. 3:11; 2 Kings 2:12; Jer. 19:3). He did it at Shiloh. He did it to Solomon's temple. He did it to Nehushtan. He did it to Herod's temple. And the holy prophets of old used the kind of language in declaring the righteousness of such judgments that makes Cromwell's men look like dithering liberals.

The principle of new life must therefore be active and present before we can be entrusted with any element of public worship, whether high, low, or middle. The Spirit creates the church, *not the other way around*, and when that Spirit-created living water is there, we must find a cistern for it. But finding a cistern is not the same thing as finding the water. The history of the church is littered with people who have made this damning mistake. Woe to those who have committed two evils.

"For my people have committed two evils; they have forsaken me the fountain of living waters, and hewed them out cisterns, broken cisterns, that can hold no water" (Jer. 2:13).

So we must see Christ, and we must see Him with evangelical eyes. We must do this before forming any dogmatic convictions about liturgy whatever. Before taking on the role of a liturgist, whether amateur or professional, we must pass our prelims. Our board consists of Martyn Lloyd-Jones, Charles Spurgeon, Charles Simeon, and a couple of hot-gospelers from the Kentucky frontier. Their appointed task is not to fence the font, or the Table, but rather our right to make contributions to the liturgical discussions.

Men love rituals. Man is a liturgy-making creature. Nothing whatever can be done about it—the only thing that distinguishes one tribe from another is the respective shape of their rituals. But every tribe has them. Some are ornate, and others are simpler, but they are all there. This sign or that one, this tablecloth or that one, three candlesticks or none, and so on. Liturgy is inescapable.

But the thing that distinguishes the regenerate from the unregenerate is something quite different, and this distinguishing mark is what I call true evangelical faith. This is the understanding—an understanding down in the bones—that the Spirit moves where and how He wills. We cannot whistle Him up, and we cannot make Him do tricks.

Men want to distinguish between true and false, right and wrong, on the basis of what is going on *out there*—instead of remembering that a true Jew is one inwardly. Circumcision is of the heart, by the Spirit. It is the same with baptism. True *baptism* is of the internal man, by the Holy Spirit, and if that is missing you do not have a Christian inwardly. You do not have a true Christian, but rather a wet member of the visible covenant. The only thing *we* control (with the variations we have in our rituals) is *how* wet that member of the visible covenant is. And there an unregenerate Baptist has a clear advantage over an unregenerate Presbyterian.

Because of how men love rituals, they can co-opt, with relative ease, a God-given ritual. God gave the law of Moses, and the people constantly had to be told that God wanted mercy, not sacrifice. "So why'd you give us *sacrifices* then?" the unregenerate mutter. God gave them the bronze serpent, a type of the Lord Jesus, which had to be destroyed by another type of the Lord Jesus. And God gave us the Lord's Supper, and we quickly (within the first century) figured out a way for that Supper to do us more harm than good (1 Cor. 11:17). So there is no automatic blessing that can come to us from the outside created world.

We can only be blessed in our religious activities if the Holy Spirit has given us a new hearts. A new heart can come through the ordinances of God (hearing the Word, prayers, the sacraments, etc.) in true evangelical faith. But without that true evangelical faith, all religious activity is just so many drowning swimmers clutching at their anvils.

———

This is why any liturgical emphasis on the externals of worship, coupled with a drifting away from historic evangelical verities (i.e., the absolute necessity of the new birth), is particularly dangerous. This point is in no way minimized by pointing out that cultural or nominal evangelicals have done exactly the same thing with the inanity of their low rituals. This does not minimize the point, but rather heightens it.

Neither is the point blunted by those who (in the name of the truth I am advocating) have turned themselves into evangelical mystic ghosts, in no need of the external world. But even they have their rudimentary rituals, and the plain teaching of Scripture goes on to silence them. Regeneration enables us to use biblical ordinances rightly; it does not eliminate the need for them. It only eliminates the spiritually stupid use of them.

If we can make this mistake with *any* external arrangement (and we most certainly can), then what is needed is a revival of the Holy Spirit, blowing wherever He wants to. When He does this, the first thing to topple is every form of sanctimonious religiosity. So instead of building so many liturgical mobile home parks, we really ought to be praying for a Category 5 revival.

———

I once heard a friend make a wonderful point in a sermon. He pointed out the reason Jesus resisted those who believed in Him at the end of John 2 and how this helps explain His treatment of Nicodemus in John 3.

"But Jesus did not commit himself unto them, because he knew all men, And needed not that any should testify of man: for he knew what was in man. There was a man of the Pharisees, named Nicodemus" (John 2:24–3:1).

He knew what was in man, and *there was a man . . .*

This is why we have to be born again, and this is why the Spirit has to do it. Whenever we do it, our reformations consist of changing the tablecloth. There. *That* should please Him.

———

There is a temptation for those Christians who want to emphasize ritual (in the wrong way) to say that in the new covenant, things are all different because of the way Christ is present in His worship now. But this overlooks several things. First, Christ has *always* been present with His people. The Rock that accompanied Israel was Christ (1 Cor. 10:4), and the people then drank spiritual drink and ate spiritual food.

The second point unfolds from the first. We are not permitted to draw contrasts where the New Testament draws parallels. The Corinthians were tempted to put on airs over against the Jews. *We* have spiritual food. *We* have spiritual drink. So did the Jews, Paul replies bluntly. You can have religious ceremonial, God-given ritual, whole burnt offerings and sacrifices, baptism in the cloud and sea, and still be overthrown in the wilderness (1 Cor. 10:5). You can have a degree in liturgics and still not have the one thing needful (Heb. 4:2). Not only is it possible to do this, it is *easy* to do this. The human soul *likes* making this mistake. And why do I talk this way? Because the Bible does, over and over again. It is never rude to speak biblically.

So if we look at this carefully, we see that the Golden Rule is another way of expressing the duties of love. Jesus said that He did not come to abolish the law and the prophets, but rather to fulfill them (Matt. 5:17). This is how He does that—by giving a heart of love, by giving the kind of heart that understands the Golden Rule.

He gives the new heart. He converts the soul. He opens our eyes. He makes light shine out of darkness. He pours out the spirit of regeneration. He gives us true evangelical faith, the only catalyst that can make any religious activity whatever acceptable in the sight of God (Heb. 4:3).

Apart from the new birth, God hates whatever it is we think we are doing. Away with the noise of your songs! High church, low church, stand-on-the-yellow-line church . . . God spews it out of His mouth.

AGAINST THE SACRAMENTS

THE REVEREND CONFECTIONERS IN THE BACK of the Westminster Candy Shop one day decided to change the recipes because customers were no longer buying the Sawdust Swirl. But rather than continuing with their experiments, they took a vote and decided to return to the original recipes that had been in use when the shop first opened three and a half centuries before. Unfortunately, the managers of the shop viewed these events with deep suspicion and declared the Reformation Fudge Supreme to be both fattening and heretical.

———

The sacraments are visible signs given to us by God to declare that salvation is from His hand alone. We (naturally) like to use the sacraments in such a way as to invert the meaning and declare our independence from Him. We need to learn how to make the same distinctions that are easy to make when talking about the Scriptures. If we say that we are saved on the basis of the Bible alone, we are not making any claims about the paper, the ink, and the leather or the maps, concordance, and ribbons. In the same way we are not saved by water, or by bread and wine. The surgeon may pick up many different instruments in the course of the operation, but it is the surgeon who is doing it. If we have mastered this distinction, we stand against every form of sacramental superstition and abuse.

A pastor friend once tweeted this: "Sometimes a pastor needs to take a man's baptism and trash it and bury it in front of him and only then will it become true."[5] The reaction he got illustrated the need for such comments to multiply and increase. But why would a *pastor* say something like that? Aren't we supposed to be ministers of Word and sacrament? Why would we ever want to trash something that we are ministers of?

We trash the sacraments, if and when we do, *because* we are ministers of the Word. We trash the Word, if and when we do, *because* we are ministers of the sacraments. We live this way because this is what Scripture, taken in its entirety, requires of us.

We may only trash such things if unbelief and superstition have already trashed them.

"The sacrifice of the wicked is an abomination to the Lord: But the prayer of the upright is his delight" (Prov. 15:8).

God delights in the prayer of the upright, but if a man is wicked, he cannot buy God off through showing up with a sacrifice. Not only does God not receive such a sacrifice, He regards it with loathing. The word *abomination* is a strong one here—the sacrifices and liturgical observances of a wicked man cause God to recoil in disgust. And if God recoils in disgust, shouldn't we also? The sacraments are sacrifices of praise, are they not? And what does God think of such sacrifices from the wicked?

A wicked man, just being what he is, presents abominable sacrifices. But wait, he can even make it worse—if he comes with evil intent brewing in his mind actively, how much more of an abomination it becomes.

---

5 Toby Sumpter, Twitter post, July 1, 2012, 5:18 p.m., http://twitter.com/TJSumpter.

"The sacrifice of the wicked is *abomination*: How much more, when he bringeth it with a wicked mind?" (Prov. 21:27).

To desire the sacrifices (and the sacraments) to be *automatically* a good thing is to forget the covenantal realities. It is to forget that the world is governed by a *personal* God. It is an attempt to keep Christ in a box. The heart of man is fully capable of polluting whatever he might be offering to God. He does this whenever he thinks that believing the promises and keeping God on a short rope are the same thing.

"He that turneth away his ear from hearing the law, even his prayer shall be abomination" (Prov. 28:9).

This would include prayers at the baptismal font, and prayers offered over the eucharistic celebration, would it not?

So this is why a minister might want to trash a man's baptism, or his diligence in communing, or his Bible study skills, or his theological acumen, or his prayer warrior status, or his tithing prowess, or his clerical garb . . . age. Why? So that it might rot in the ground, and rise again to newness of life.

———

These truths can be seen in a type. The law of God distinguished between clean and unclean animals—the unclean could not be offered up in sacrifice. From this, some might want to infer that any clean animal could be so offered, but this was not the case at all. An animal could belong to the category of the clean, and yet still not be fit for sacrifice. The weak and infirm animals could not be offered, the animals with a blemish could not be, and so on.

When we come to worship God, we come to offer *ourselves*. In the sacraments, we are partaking. Baptism represents our union with Christ, and the Lord's Supper our partaking of Christ. We are involved, and *we* are involved as part of the offering. Now if someone is baptized, this means he is a covenantal sheep, not a dog. But more is required than "not being a dog." When a priest was examining an animal presented for sacrifice, his work was not done when he ascertained that it was not a dog.

And of course, the final gospel answer is that we are all of us maimed, and the only perfect sacrifice was that offered by the only clean victim. If we are in Him, then His perfections are ours. If not, then our imperfections remain our own—even if we have been removed by baptism from the category of the unclean.

A blemished sheep in sacrifice can no more be accepted by God than a pig can.

——

The alternative to believing in the real presence of the Lord in the Supper is believing in His real absence. *That* can't be right. So perhaps a better way to frame the debate should therefore be local presence versus a rightly understood *covenantal* presence.

One of the great problems with local presence has to do with space (the Lord's body being *there*, on the table), but it also is problematic with regard to time. God's promises, being covenantal, include all time, history, lives, genealogies, biographies, and the last day. The Lord's Supper has to be understood *in the story*. The promises concern the video, not the snapshot. We must be opposed to every sacrament caught in a freeze frame. In order to be true sacraments, they must be story sacraments. And what is the story?

We partake of the Lord in the participles, we partake of Him in the partaking. We cannot say, "Look, there is the Lord, stationary, on the table." Rather, we say, "Here is the Lord *in the action* of eating and drinking." And these actions are part of a *series* of actions, which together constitute the story. We partake of the Lord's body and blood in a glorious series of verbs—declaring, praying, blessing, setting apart, taking, breaking, taking, and giving.[6] And each moment in the story says something about the end of the story.

When God speaks to us, He speaks to us about the continuation and conclusion of our story.

"And the very God of peace sanctify you wholly; and I pray God your whole spirit and soul and body be preserved blameless unto the coming of our Lord Jesus Christ. Faithful is he that calleth you, who also will do it" (1 Thess. 5:23–24).

"Being confident of this very thing, that he which hath begun a good work in you will perform it until the day of Jesus Christ" (Phil. 1:6).

So our prayer should not just be for the Lord to show up in the sacraments *now*. We want Him to come to us in salvation, of course, and—this is crucial—we want Him to *stay*. We plead with Him to *remain*. And this is what He has promised His elect that He will do. First, consider how we ask . . .

"Do not hide Your face from me; Do not turn Your servant away in anger; You have been my help; Do not leave me nor forsake me, O God of my salvation" (Ps. 27:9).

The Lord does not just promise to be with His worshipers in the moment, but rather to be with them at the Last Day. That is the promise, and that is why only evangelical faith can receive such a promise. Sacramental superstitions are up to the snapshot challenge—superstition can give the sensation of a god presenting himself *now*. But only someone who is born again can understand a promise like this one.

"Let your conduct be without covetousness; be content with such things as you have. For He Himself has said, 'I will never leave you nor forsake you.' So we may boldly say: 'The Lord is my helper; I will not fear. What can man do to me?'" (Heb. 13:5–6).

---

6 *The Westminster Confession of Faith* (Edinburgh: T & T Clark, 1881), 29.3.

If God has promised anyone that He will come to us, and that He will never go away from us, to whom is that promise made? It is a promise that encompasses the whole story—and it is therefore a promise to those for whom the whole story was written in the first place. It is for the little flock, and only for them.

"But rather seek ye the kingdom of God; and all these things shall be added unto you. *Fear not, little flock*; for it is your Father's good pleasure *to give you the kingdom*" (Luke 12:31–32).

The one who has promised is faithful, and He will do it. So if you believe, it was always yours. If you do not believe, then where is your complaint? You never wanted it anyway.

———

This is the beginning of all spiritual wisdom. Among the sons of Sarah, we find sons of both Sarah and Hagar. Among the Jews, we find Jews and Gentiles. Among the sons of Abraham, we find the sons of Abraham and Belial. Among the regenerate, we find the regenerate and the unregenerate. Among the elect, we find the elect and the reprobate. Among the baptized, we find the unbaptized. Among the communicants, we find those who refuse to commune. Until the resurrection, why do these two categories *always* arise?

———

Against the sacraments? Well, to be honest, we should only be against the makeshift, temporary ones. If it is not a sacramental observance on the part of the elect, enabling them to partake eternally in the everlasting decree, then to Hell with it.

AGAINST INFANT ANYTHING

THE SEMINARY INSTRUCTOR LEANED against his desk and asked if there were any questions. One hand went up.

"So you are saying that infant baptism dates from the earliest years of the church, and that is one of your reasons for accepting it?"

"*One* of the reasons, yes."

"But then the readings you have had us do demonstrated that the church held wildly erroneous views of baptism for over a thousand years after that?"

"I think that is a fair summary of the reading, yes."

The student came to the point he wanted to press. "So how is that an argument *for* doing it?"

"By pointing out that the babies were not the only infants."

"Okay, you lost me."

"The church was an infant when *it* was baptized, and there was a lot of growing up that had to be done. The doctrine of infant baptism was an infant when *it* was baptized, and it had a troubled childhood, especially in the junior high years."

Silence fell over the classroom. The questioner scratched his head. Finally he broke the silence. "Are there office hours this week?"

Historic evangelicals, at their best, are unaccredited teachers in the schools of the prophets. At their worst, they are sons of Zedekiah, selling little miniature horns of iron on the teevee for $9.95 plus shipping and handling (1 Kings 22:11). Institutional Christians, let us call them, at their best, are like Jehoiada (2 Kings 11:17). At their worst, they carry on in such a way as to make even a Bach chorale obnoxious to God (Amos 5:23), processing up the center aisle in such a way as to make every true child of Father want to throw a Scottish psalter at their pointy hats.

———

After baptism has taken place, everything else is part of Christian discipleship—teaching the baptized to obey all that Christ commanded. Discipleship is irreducibly, a matter of obedience, not theological test-passing. It is an ethical response, not a cognitive one. Now a certain cognitive element is necessarily there, and it obviously grows over time, but the first thing you must be after is a willingness and eagerness in the disciple to be accepted, grown, taught, and disciplined, etc. What is the point of communing a child, if that child is not growing up into righteous, peace and joy (Rom. 14:17)? Why would a minister of Christ want to give children little damnation wafers? The fact that it is the cup of *blessing* did not keep profane Corinthians from dying as they drank it. Those who practice child communion, therefore, are running the risk of incurring one of the Lord's most fearful curses (Matt. 18:6).

———

Those who object to infant baptism because of the invitation it presents to nominalism and presumption have a strong argument. If circumcision was the precursor to baptism, as paedobaptists like to argue, then the temptations that came with circumcision will also come with infant baptism. The apostle Paul tells the Roman church not to fall into presumption the way the Jews did (Rom. 11:18), and so it will not do to answer the Baptists by maintaining that infant baptism presents no temptation to presumption at all. If that were true, the biblical argument for paedobaptism would collapse. It will not do to say that the new covenant has full continuity when it comes to the privileges of the covenant, and no continuity when it comes to the responsibilities.

Baptist parents who bring up their children in the nurture and admonition of the Lord are honorary paedobaptists—however much they dislike the accolade (Rom. 2:26). They are like the son in the parable who says he will not go, and then he does (Matt. 21:28–31). Paedobaptists who bring up their children in the kind of serenity that only high presumption can provide are the other son. And, as it turns out, that other son, the one with the big talk, has an uncircumcised and unbaptized heart.

That fearful curse may be activated in more than one way. Child communionists like to point out that to refuse the elements to children is to refuse them Christ. But how does it improve matters if we bring them to Christ *thoughtlessly*?

At Christ Church, the little children are included in our worship services. They come every week, and eventually they start picking up: "These are my people. We're worshiping God." They start to learn the Doxology. They lift their hands for the Gloria Patri. They enthusiastically shout *amen*!

And when they're somewhere around a year old, they start to notice that everyone else is taking bread. When they begin to reach for the bread, and you have to hold the bread away from them, that moment has become didactic. If the lesson is "We're in and you're out," that's contrary to the statement we made at their baptism that they're in with the rest of us. So we encourage parents to begin at that point to give them the elements accompanied by teaching: "This is the body of Jesus. He died for you. He paid for your sins." In this way, they are learning from the earliest age to know that they are included and how to be a communicant member.

This practice, however, should not be perceived as a low-bar cognitive admittance test. We are not after understanding first, so that children may be admitted to the company of those who have passed their ecclesiastical prelims. Rather what we want with children who are taking the Supper is gladness, so that the right kind of understanding will then be able to *grow*.

We are treating little children as disciples, and the first lesson of every disciple is joy. "I was *glad* when they said unto me, Let us go into the house of the LORD" (Ps. 122:1). If the children are not glad to be there, then everything after that is counterproductive. When we want the children "tracking" as we commune, we are wanting them to participate in the joy— the way my one-year-old granddaughter claps after everybody sings "Happy Birthday" to one of the cousins. What we want is "Yay, here we are with Jesus again!", not an infant's contemplation of Turretin's rejection of consubstantiation on the one hand, and the folly of the Socinians on the other.

―――

Now it is quite true that an Israelite could have been saved from the Passover Angel of the Lord at the first Passover in a condition of unbelief, provided there was some blood on the door post. This was because the Lord needed to have some covenantal unbelievers around to slay in the wilderness later so that we might have *their* objective example before our eyes. Yes, they drank from the Rock that was Christ. Yes, they ate the bread from Heaven, who was Christ. What did *that* get them? Without true, living, thriving evangelical faith in Jesus, it got them an unmarked tomb in the wilderness that the archaeologists will never find. But if we could find such a grave, it would be a fitting place for certain sacramentalists to seek out as a place for a pilgrimage, in order to meditate on their futile ways.

———

Before I came to accept the need for child communion, one of my stated concerns was that those who commune children might confound things when a child's sullenness, bad attitude, or resistance to a life of joy began to be clearly manifest to everybody. That would be the signal for the "objectivists" to rush to his defense anyway. Such would separate the privileges of discipleship from the responsibilities of it. That way lies presumption, and it was the sin that the apostle Paul expressly warned those of us with a high sacramentology about (Rom. 11:18–20). You don't support the root, Mr. Sacrament Man, the root supports you. And you maintain your connection to the root, the apostle went on to say, by internalizing in your disposition, in your soul, in your joy, what the Larger Catechism has to say about justifying faith.[7] Look it up.

———

This is Westminsterian joy in the heart, not Westminsterian theology in the head. If you cultivate the former, you will have the latter, but they must go in that order. If you have the latter only, then you have the ironic spectacle of "evangelical" Calvinists making their kids score ninety percent or above

———

7　*The Westminster Larger Catechism* (Lindenhurst, NY: Great Christian Books, 2013), Question 72.

on the grace portion of their theology exams before they give them some grace as a reward. But the solution to *that* appalling business is not to reject or set aside the authority of grace to shape our lives in joy.

Salvation first, and then the theology of it. Joy at the foundation, and then the building. Jesus first, then the discussions.

———

Faith is a faculty, but it is not a faculty that comes and goes. It is not a discrete faculty, or a solitary organ. I also have no problem with a description of faith that sees it as a characteristic of a life lived over time. Faith does not come out of a "faith box," but rather comes from the heart of a man.

———

When my baptist friends cheer me on, it is because they agree with my evangelicalism. They are bewildered by what I will do with the babies. When my paedobaptist friends do not cheer me on, it is because they are drifting away from that evangelicalism. They like what I do with the babies, for the most part, but they want it grounded in a different theology.

———

Why does one covenant child grow up loving Jesus, and another, just as baptized and just as communed, grow up despising Him? The answer is the new birth, about which more later. It is not having an "imparted faculty" inside you, as a distinct faculty. It is a matter of having an imparted *heart*.

If there are only two final destinations, Heaven or Hell, and there are, and if it is possible for baptized Christians, who have been communing since they were "so high," with all their external papers in order, to go to Hell, and it is, and if God is sovereign over all history (which includes every biography), which He is, then we must have a robust doctrine of heart regeneration. It is the only way to make sense of the basic data.

This is why I hold that true faith in Jesus is a faculty. It is a faculty or characteristic of a regenerate heart. Unregenerate hearts have the same faculty called "faith," but because they are still (by nature) objects of wrath, that faculty is directed toward one or more idols. We accept covenant children as having a true heart of faith, and we teach them how to grow from immature faith to a more mature faith, unless and until works of the flesh make their lack of regeneration manifest to all.

———

Our baptist brothers see the problem, and (in my view) want to uproot the tares before it is time. They wind up damaging the wheat. The sacramentalists, I believe, are too careless about letting everything grow together, until eventually, like the Episcopal Church, they think that morning glory is wheat. And why shouldn't we ordain this morning glory as a bishop? His relationship with the ragweed is a mutually affirming and caring relationship.

———

What I am after is an institutional church with an evangelical heart. I am at war with false dichotomies. It need not be sectarian to be evangelical, and it need not be formalist to be a church instead of a sect. That said, communing children from a very young age is not *necessarily* the road to formalism—but it is a good way to get there if you want.

———

Despite the concerns of some, there is nothing whatever semi-Marcionite about this position of evangelical child communion. How can it be a rejection of the authority of the

Old Testament to take to heart all the authoritative examples and warnings from the Old Testament? The Old Testament demands a unity of heart and external worship. God desires mercy, not sacrifice. To obey is better than sacrifice. Sacrifices and burnt offerings God did not require, but a humble and contrite heart. Rend your hearts, not your garments. Circumcise your hearts therefore. These were not things that Marcion could understand. Had he understood them, he would not have rejected the Word of God.

And neither is it any form of recognizable gnosticism. There is nothing esoteric or utopian about what I am urging. I do not believe that regeneration is a mystery spark, hidden down deep in our hearts. Rather, it is the result of God's supernatural work, by which He restores *nature*. The transformation of the water at Cana was a supernatural act, but it did not have a supernatural result. Jesus made natural wine, not supernatural ambrosia, but He nevertheless did it by supernatural means. In the new birth, God makes a new man out of an old one; He makes a true man out of a wrecked one. He doesn't create heavenly fairies. *God by His supernatural power restores nature.*

A child who is communed without partaking of that restoration is actually experiencing a sacramental wrecking ball, one that makes him even more of a ruin than before.

———

Sure, there are evangelicals out there who are functionally gnostics, who have imbued their priests (e.g., summer camp counselors) with mysterious powers. Here, pray this prayer, throw the pine cone into the fire, and the divine spark is kindled within. But, of course, there are sacramentalists who are every bit as gnostic. They have imbued their priests (e.g., priests) with mysterious powers. Here, eat this wafer, and the divine mystery starts within. One says *mumbo* and the other says *jumbo*. But to insist that the recipient is receiving extra "gnosis" through the ritual, despite all appearances, despite the life lived, is also gnosticism. Some gnostics use rituals and some use formulas. So what? What they have in common is their refusal to integrate their "mystery," whatever it is, with this life, this history, *this* biography.

So it is not gnostic to insist (pastorally) on an integrated life, one where the inner and outer man increasingly line up. It is not gnostic to shepherd little children (whom Christ has welcomed), teaching and urging them to live faithfully as disciples—for that is what they are. But as real disciples, one of the foundational things they must learn is the lesson which Nicodemus had somehow missed: *You must be born again.* Wanting covenant children to grow up enjoying the blessing of God in practice (and not just on paper) is the commanded blending of earthy and heavenly, inner and outer, heart and body, physical and spiritual.

AGAINST TRADITION

"May I please come in?" the new wine said.

The old wineskin looked at the new wine with eyes kind of squinty. "I am not sure that would be entirely wise."

"Nevertheless, that is my request."

"Would you promise to be good?"

"I can promise to act according to my nature."

"That is what I am afraid of," said the old wineskin.

"It is good for new wine to be new wine," said the new wine.

"Yes, it is good for the new wine to be new wine, but this is only good *for* the new wine. My question concerns whether it is good for the old wineskin."

"That I cannot say," said the new wine. "I am new around here."

"I don't know either," said the old wineskin. "The last time I had any new wine in me was back when I was a new wineskin. Ah, those were the days . . . I remember one time when Machen . . ."

"Excuse me," the new wine said. "May I come in?"

"Yes, you may. But I don't want you to make the presbytery blow up—the floor would be sticky for weeks."

"I'll do my best."

"That's all we can expect."

"Will the rest of the old wineskin do its best too?"

"I am afraid that is asking bit too much."

———

A shrewd old pastor once said, with a glint in his eye, "We Baptists don't believe in tradition. It's contrary to our historic position." All churches have traditions, and the older they are, the more pernicious they are. We should never forget that Cain was the eldest. If he had founded one, his church would have had the very best claim on antiquity. The choice is not between tradition and no tradition, but rather tradition as rightly handled by both adjectives and adverbs, and tradition wrongly handled by them. In other words, there can be wrong tradition, rightly handled, right tradition, wrongly handled, and so forth.

———

> Hearken to me, ye that follow after righteousness, ye that seek the Lord: Look unto the rock whence ye are hewn, And to the hole of the pit whence ye are digged. Look unto Abraham your father, And unto Sarah that bare you: For I called him alone, And blessed him, and increased him. (Isa. 51:1–2)

> And think not to say within yourselves, We have Abraham to our father: for I say unto you, that God is able of these stones to raise up children unto Abraham. (Matt. 3:9)

To the unconverted heart, it appears as though God trifles with us. He tells the Jews specifically to look to Abraham, and then John the Baptist says that looking to Abraham is no great shakes. Isaiah tells them to look to Sarah, and then the apostle Paul tells a bunch of them that doing what they were told actually made them sons of Hagar (Gal. 4:24).

To the unconverted heart it sure looks that way. To the converted heart, the distance between looking to Abraham and looking to Abraham is as vast as the distance between Heaven and Hell. There is a chasm between the two, and the bosom of Abraham on only one side of it.

———

Life is right at the center of God's purposes for this dead world of ours. But the way into this new world He is fashioning is quite similar to the way we got into the old world—we have to be born into it. A new world, a new creation, requires, of necessity, a new birth. How will the new world get *people* otherwise?

But this new world is being established in the midst of the old house—it is like a remodel project in a house, but with nobody moving out while the work is in progress. The end result will be a completely new house, and there is some debris in the meantime, and you can see aspects of the old house disappearing, and the shape of the new house is becoming clearer, and the whole thing is quite exciting.

Material from the old house can and usually does go into the new house—which is how we are to keep tradition alive—but in order for that to happen, it must be made new, it must be made alive. The old material has to become new material in order to go into the new house. This is the meaning of the new birth. And the transformation is no incidental or surface thing—it is not a matter of sanding, or painting, or carving. No, the dead stones are turned into living stones (1 Pet. 2:4–5), which of necessity affects everything about the stone, except the fact that it is stone. Stone, but stone that is alive now, which is not exactly a trifle. So not only is this a remodel project, but it is one in which the house is in the process of becoming a living organism.

———

Now all churches have distinctives, and ours is no exception. We believe certain things are true and not other things, and we organize our worship services in a particular way and not in another way, and so on. In our case, some examples would be that we practice a weekly renewal of the covenant, which means that each service culminates with communion. We are postmillennial, which means that we believe that the world will be successfully evangelized before the Lord comes again. We sing psalms and hymns, which means that we believe our music should be God-honoring and rich in fiber. We believe in cultural engagement, which means that we hold the Christian faith is not a private mystery religion, but rather a public faith, claiming that the authority of Jesus Christ must be universally recognized by all nations.

We hope to pass all these traditions on to our children, and to their children after them. But how could *that* ever happen? This brings us back to the centrality of the new birth. Without the new birth, all the doctrinal and liturgical work in the world is just the reorganization of dead materials, instead of what it is described in the Bible as being, which is the organization and discipleship of living materials.

Liturgy without life is like putting makeup on a corpse. Doctrine without this same life is like spelling everything right on the tombstone.

The dead are great at keeping tradition. Nothing ever changes.

Without the principle of new life, nothing matters anyway. With this principle of new life, brought about by men preaching a robust gospel, and expecting results in faith as they do, all these other issues, these other distinctives, become important in their own order and in their proper time. Once your newborn daughter is out of the ICU and home safely from the hospital, it is *then* appropriate to think about getting her violin lessons in due course.

We have to be adults in our thinking of course. There are many "evangelicals" who have experienced the gift of this new life, and who emphasize it as they ought, but who have hired a terrible violin instructor. And others, reacting against that, have assumed that the life principle is somehow optional, so long as the violin instructor is a virtuoso.

———

Jesus Christ wants those who believe and understand these things to assume the center. He prohibits us *seizing* the center—the kingdom of God is not like a coup. The new life has political results but is not achieved by political means, which, incidentally, includes ecclesiastical politics. The experience of the new life will always, of necessity, be at the very center of God's work in the world, because that is what He is doing here. And the intelligent awareness of what He is doing (which is only by faith, from first to last) will always be at the center of that experience. This is just another way of saying that the center of gravity in this new world that God is fashioning is, of necessity, an evangelical center.

So we know what God's plan for this world is—it is life from the dead. He has told us this quite plainly. God's plan is a resurrection plan. This means that if our plans are to line up with His, we have got to put the principle of new life right at the foundation of all we want to do. And, by the grace of God's Spirit, we are seeking to do just that.

"For God, who commanded the light to shine out of darkness, hath shined in our hearts, to give the light of the knowledge of the glory of God in the face of Jesus Christ" (2 Cor. 4:6).

———

This means that the central tradition that must be passed on to our children, and their children after them, is the long and honored evangelical tradition of rising from the dead.

———

I was sitting in a conference talk once and a phrase just popped into my head. That phrase was "the expulsive power of a new affection." I thought initially it might be something from Jonathan Edwards, but when I looked it up, it turned out to be a sermon title from Thomas Chalmers—which I then read. Good stuff.

Before telling you how it connects (everything), allow me to summarize Chalmers's point. He was arguing that moralism cannot motivate men and women to live properly simply by disparaging the vanity and evanescence of the world. Offering such disparagement is easy to do, and the folly of the world can be made thoroughly obvious, but still nothing changes. In order for something to actually change, there must be a "new affection" implanted, which happens to an individual at conversion.

The reason the world can be effectively disparaged and yet worldlings don't change is because they have no way to change. They are like Peter, only in reverse. He told Jesus, when he was asked if he was going to depart also, that he had nowhere to go. "Then Simon Peter answered him, Lord, to whom shall we go? thou hast the words of eternal life" (John 6:68).

Chalmers argued that the human soul must have an object of affection. It is an iron law of our constitutional makeup. We cannot stop setting our affections on *something*—and if all we have is the world, it will be something in the world. If all we have is three straws, it will be one of those three straws. If someone comes along and points out that setting your affections on straws is "dumb and stupid," you might agree with that observation entirely. But you still wouldn't be able to do anything else because that is all you have. Where else can you go?

In order for anything to change, there must be a new affection. Christ must be offered through the gospel, and Christ must be *loved*. When He is loved, we then see the expulsive power of a new affection—the things that were necessarily dear before (even though acknowledged by the one who loved them as stupid vanity) are expelled to the outer darkness. Thus far Chalmers.

Let us say there is some major house cleaning that needs to occur in a church. There are a few folks at Sardis who have kept their garments clean (Rev. 3:4), but the spiritual condition of the rest of the place is *meh*. There needs to be a corporate demonstration of the expulsive power of a new affection. But that new affection has to be more than just present. It has to be out there. Jesus has to be loved and praised and talked about.

I am convinced that we have plenty of Christians, carriers of this new affection. But for various reasons, we are chary of "unleashing it." In corporate settings, this expulsive power is experienced (often) as a convulsive power first. And that is just one reason why we are jumpy about it. But Paul tells us how to behave in this regard.

"Do all things without murmurings and disputings: That ye may be blameless and harmless, the sons of God, without rebuke, in the midst of a crooked and perverse nation, among whom ye shine as lights in the world; Holding forth the word of life; that I may rejoice in the day of Christ, that I have not run in vain, neither laboured in vain" (Phil. 2:14–16).

The contrast of a shining light against a backdrop of darkness is not a subtle distinction. And as we shine out as lights, what are we doing? We are holding forth the word of life.

That word of life has an expulsive power. It expels death. Jesus is that expulsive power. Jesus *named* is that expulsive power. This new tradition of rising from the dead supplants the old tradition of lying in the ground.

There are some standard evangelical interpretations, hoary
with age, which are, for all that, what more careful exegetes
might call wrongity wrong wrong. A passage that comes to mind
is Revelation 3:20, commonly used as a salvation text—Jesus
is knocking at the door of your heart, and won't you pray the
prayer and ask Him in? While I don't want to be a fusser, this
kind of thing, unchecked, can become widespread, and contribute significantly to false understandings of conversion. How
many salvation prayers consist of asking Jesus into your heart, or
asking Christ into your life? Don't get me wrong—Christ *is* in us
(Col. 1:27; Rom. 8:10), but not because we asked Him in. And it
would be better to speak of Christ inviting us into His life—after
all, He is the one with any life capable of being inviting at all.

So this business of opening the door of your heart is one of
our traditions. What are we to do with it? The passage is talking
about Jesus knocking at the door of a *church* (the door of the
Laodicean church, to be precise), and if any man there assumed
the duty of a diligent porter, Christ promised to come in and
dine with him, to have table fellowship with *him*. Where this
leaves the deaf but credentialed ecclesiastical porters is a topic
for another day. They were polishing the silver communion
service in a back room, and they probably couldn't hear.

This misunderstanding about Revelation 3:20 is not the end
of the world, of course. Lots of people get saved using language that is not according to Hoyle. When I was in the Navy,
I remember one man I was witnessing to using a prayer that
went something like, "Damn it, I'm here." The real issue is that
God is a lover of heart religion, and He sees and reads what is
really going on. And as Bunyan put it, "rather let thy hearts be
without words, than thy words without a heart."[8] If your heart
is without words, God can still hear you.

---

8   From "Mr. John Bunyan's Dying Saying: Of Prayer" in *The Works of That Eminent
Servant of Christ John Bunyan, Volume 1* (Philadelphia: John Ball, 1850), 47.

———

In other instances, the handling of classic conversion texts are accurate enough as far as they go, but there is more that can be said—but not less. The "more" that can be said is usually a "more" that includes the entire church. The church is nothing without individual conversions, but the church is not nothing but individual conversions. The whole is greater than the sum of its parts. This is where the evangelical tradition goes astray.

For example, take the heart of stone, heart of flesh passage in Ezekiel 36. This promised transition was not one from faithful immaturity to glorified maturity. Rather, it is a promise of a glorious heart *conversion*—from sin to righteousness.

How does God describe Israel in this passage? They had "defiled it by their own way" (v. 17), and their sin was as "the uncleanness of a removed woman" (v. 17). God poured out His "fury" upon them for their bloodshed (v. 18), and for the pollution of their idols (v. 18). When they were scattered by God, wherever they went, the holy name of God was "profaned" because of the judgment upon them (v. 20, 22). God then promised to sprinkle them clean from all their "filthiness" (v. 25), and to cleanse them from all their "idols" (v. 25). It is at this point that He promises them a new heart, promising to replace their stony heart with a heart of flesh. That stony heart was obviously a bad bit of business.

I remember Barry McGuire once saying, in response to the charge that he had been brainwashed, something like, "That's good. My brains needed a little scrub."

———

But as with the vision of the valley of dry bones in the next chapter (Ezek. 37:11), this is a promise of *corporate* regeneration. Israel needed a new heart; Israel needed to be converted. It is for this reason that the needed conversion of covenant members ought not to be controversial among us. That is how the Christian church was born—born again, actually—at Pentecost. Converting unconverted covenant members is something that God specializes in, and we need to be careful not to resist His work by claiming it is somehow unnecessary. One of the times it is most necessary is when people have come to assume it is not necessary at all. On this rule, when Jesus came, things were in a bad way for Israel. And so in Ezekiel 36–37, and in John 3, God promises to do this work of heart conversion *en masse*.

Now the fact that He does it *en masse* does not mean that individuals are excluded. We don't want to be in the position of those who argue that Noah's flood was *global*, and therefore this individual patch of ground need not have gotten wet. We don't want to reason like those who say that the entire valley of dry bones was regenerated, and that is why we see so many individual skeletons lying about.

Jesus speaks to Nicodemus about this corporate regeneration, but He also speaks about the individual aspects of it. But even if He hadn't, the necessity of individual conversion follows from the necessity of corporate conversion by good and necessary consequence. But the Lord, being merciful, knew that we weren't very good at good and necessary consequences, and so He spelled both aspects out for us. And are we teachers in the new Israel, and we don't know these things?

Unless *a man* is born again, *he* cannot see the kingdom (John 3:3, 5). But then Jesus tells Nicodemus that "you all" must be born again (John 3:7), and He consistently uses the plural in His explanation to Nicodemus. Nicodemus was an individual who needed to be born again, but he was also a representative of all Israel. The whole nation needed regeneration, and that is what happened at Pentecost. The valley of dry bones came to life. So did the Nicodemus bones.

———

We have to understand what kind of thing life is. In the fallacy of composition, a man says that if the tank is heavy, then every individual part of it must be heavy. But it is not a fallacy to say the entire tank is made out of metal, and so this part must be metal. Now life is more like "metal" than "heavy." The Spirit is life itself, and this is why the new life in Christ does not have dead appendages.

"But ye are not in the flesh, but in the Spirit, if so be that the Spirit of God dwell in you. Now if any man have not the Spirit of Christ, he is none of his" (Rom. 8:9).

There has never been a skeleton yet who was the life of the party.

———

One more thing, anticipating a "yeah, but." When I said above that the life of Christ does not have dead appendages, some might object (rightly enough) and say that there are some illustrations in Scripture that do indicate dead appendages on a living Christ (John 15:5–6; Rom. 11:17). This is quite correct. Those illustrations are there, right alongside the illustrations that say the unconverted have nothing to do with Him ("tares, not wheat," "none of his," "never knew you," etc.).

This is why, in order to speak as the Bible speaks, we must get more comfortable with biblical paradox and less comfortable with the tidiness of our own systems. I do not say that God is contradicting Himself—all of reality is self-consistent, and God's words are silver, refined seven times. There is no dross in them. What I am saying is that *we* are going to grow up into that self-consistent revelation far more quickly if we learn what the art of divine conversation is like.

When we commune with God in this divine conversation, the first lesson is that of how to stop finishing His sentences for Him. That is a tradition we should learn.

AGAINST SYSTEMATICS

ONE NIGHT, AFTER HAVING CONSUMED FAR TOO MUCH PIZZA, an old school Presbyterian minister retired to bed. About two in the morning, after much turning and spindling up in the covers, he awoke in a sweat, and there, hovering over the foot of his bed, in a nimbus cloud of glory, was the Westminster Confession, without the American revisions. He sat bolt upright, his eyes like a couple of shiny hubcaps.

"I didn't know you were an angel!" He exclaimed. "Who knew!?"

"My son, my faithful son. I am no angel, but merely a system of sound doctrine. But as far as the seventeenth century goes, I *have* been told I won 'best in show.'"

"I should say! You're the best!"

"Nay, my son. For like all other synods and councils, whether general or particular, I may err, and have erred, and am not to be made the rule of faith or practice, but rather used as a help in both." The Confession arched her eyebrows, as much as to say that "we have been over this before."

"Not a rule of faith or practice?"

"Right. But just a help in both."

The minister was muttering into the covers, bunched up in both fists. "Beg pardon?" said the Confession.

The minister lowered his hands.

"Uh oh," he repeated.

———

The Bible says that Jesus taught with authority, and not like the scribadiddles. Since those words were first penned two thousand years ago, pastors have been trying to rehabilitate the scribal reputation, with varying degrees of success. The church has ministers—which was a gift of Jesus Christ Himself from Heaven—and the church also has a professional class, which may or may not be a gift from Heaven.

———

Jesus Christ is prophet, priest and king, eternally and forever, but many of the problems that afflict Christendom are the result of our vain attempts to divvy Him up. The activists want Him to be King, and the end result of their labors is a bunch of social justice hooey. The sacramentalists want Him just to be a High Priest, and the end result of that yearning is worship services that look like the induction of the new Director General of the Moose Lodge. And the evangelicals want to establish and run schools of the prophets out in the hinterlands, far away from the corridors of power, and the end result of *that* endeavor is that they all disappear in a puff of gnostic smoke.

If I may simplify the scriptural pattern, the sacramentalists are in the tabernacle, or the magistrates at court, doing the drill just like they thought they were told to, and then the prophets come in to tell them that it doesn't matter that they did it "just so," they still messed up. Sometimes the disobedience that they rebuke is high-handed, involving the weightier matters of the law, but other times it seems pretty mysterious. I think of the poor king who hit the floor with the arrows three times instead of five or six times, incurring Elisha's anger.

The point is that, in the Scriptures, the evangelicals out in the woods take the establishment seriously. The Tishbite is not a creature of the court, but he does come to the court with some-thing to say to them there. The Tishbite is not an establishment churchman, which thereby shows that the Word of God is not contained or bounded by the morning and evening hokey pokey of the priests. At the same time, the schools of the prophets are not ascetic communities of anabaptist or essence commandoes, living in serene detachment from the corruptions of "the world." And then, just to keep us on our toes, sometimes the king is a prophet (David), and sometimes a churchman is (Samuel).

Without the evangelicals, the churchmen will put the whole thing on cruise control, and declare to the great congregation that God don't make no junk, and is very, very happy with all of them. But without the institutional church, the evangel-icals are like a detached conscience floating aimlessly above the Great Plains somewhere. What is the point of a conscience with no body?

And in church history, occasionally, like a blue comet on holiday with no schedule to keep, a lonely figure will appear who appears to function fluidly in all three realms, making it look easy. Chesterton was like that. Worldview thinking radi-ated from him like heat from a stove. That is what systematic thinking should look like, but it hardly ever does.

True, integrated worldview thinking runs like Eric Liddell, stretched out, feeling God's pleasure. We like what we see, and so we organize imitative worldview thinking seminars, in which we train college-bound kids how to run three-legged races at the church picnic.

———

Systematic theology is nothing less than remembering what you read in other passages while you are reading *this* passage. The kind of thing that gives systematic theology a bad name is remembering what you *thought* other passages said, privileging them in some form of special pleading, and making the verse in front of you do little poodle tricks.

Illegitimate systematics is done by the kind of people who put together jigsaw puzzles with a pair of scissors and a mallet handy. The solution is not to abandon systematics, which is not possible anyway. Everybody in this discussion has a system because everybody wants to understand what the Bible as a whole teaches. Our task is nevertheless to guard ourselves against Procrustean interpretations, and we do this best by acknowledging frankly that *every* school of thought will have such temptations. This happens when we get certain passages "down" and then feel impelled to protect that understanding against the evil stratagems of problem passages.

A theological breakthrough occurs when a systematic proposal is made which "saves the phenomena" for a greater number of passages, and which greatly reduces the temptations for special pleading. This is why I consider the understanding of the objectivity of the covenant to be a theological breakthrough. The Calvinist passages concern the decrees and sovereignty of God, and they stand as is, and the Arminian passages concern our participation in the covenant, from which it is possible for nonelect covenant members to fall away. The decrees are real, and no one can lay a charge against God's elect, and the covenant is also real, so all baptized Christians need to take care lest they fall from from grace.

We maintain balance by holding fast to both poles—we don't try to go down the black diamond run of sovereignty and free will with just one ski on our right foot and one pole in our left hand.

———

In order to maintain this balance, we have to hold fast to two distinct sets of dichotomies. The first is on the covenantal side, where we take seriously everything God says about the distinction between the world and the church, between the unbaptized and the baptized, between unbelievers and believers, and between visible pagans and visible saints. The second is the distinction we must make *within* the covenant between those who *say* they are and those who *are*. There are Christians and there are Christians indeed. You know you are on the right track when you are accused of contradicting what you just said in the first set of distinctions, but it is no contradiction at all. There is a distinction between the common operations of the Spirit, which are no less real for being temporary, and the sealing and earnest of the Spirit, which cannot be touched by height, breadth, or depth, or things present or things to come.

If you make the covenantal warnings disappear under the shadow of the decrees, then you run the risk of becoming a Greek fatalist instead of a Scots Calvinist. If you put the decrees up for grabs by foregrounding the covenant signs (like baptism), then you run the risk of becoming a German Lutheran instead of a Dutch Calvinist. I only bring ethnicities in to see if I can inflame this thing further.

—

In sum, everything the Bible says about the distinction between the church and the world is true, and everything the Bible says about the distinction between the regenerate church and the unregenerate church is true. Unregenerate church? Has Wilson, as Wodehouse might ask, gone off his onion?

Not at all. Just lay out all the verses, all of them, and throw away your scissors and mallet. Let the Scriptures speak.

—

After warning about the bad dudes Hymenaeus and Philetus, whose words were a canker, increasing to more ungodliness, consisting as they did of profane and vain babbling, Paul says this about the house of the Lord:

"But in a great house there are not only vessels of gold and of silver, but also of wood and earth; and some to honor, and some to dishonor. If a man therefore purge himself from these, he shall be a vessel unto honor, sanctified, and meet for the master's use, and prepared unto every good work" (2 Tim. 2:20–21).

First, let us dispatch the idea that "purge himself" affects anything. Men repent and God gives repentance. Men harden their hearts and God hardens them. Men believe and God gives faith. Men love and God gives love. Nothing different here. To be changed from one kind of vessel to another requires the efficacious grace of God and, if that regenerating grace is given, it will be the man who repents and cleanses himself.

———

So if you baptize a chamber pot, what is it still full of? To be *in* the great house is a very different question from what kind of vessel you are in that house. So, I would argue, the two sets of categories I am setting forth are categories found *in the text itself*. In this illustration, we have the categories of inside and outside the great house, and then we have the categories of dishonorable vessels inside and honorable vessels inside.

Take these categories in order to believe them all, affirm them all, and preach them all. This is what a spurious systematic refuses to do.

———

In recent years, it has become *de rigeur* to say that the stories of the Bible ought not to be read in ways that reduce the message to simple little Sunday School lessons. And of course, as with all such things, there is a sense in which this is perfectly acceptable, and, in certain ways, a necessary corrective. The

Bible is not Aesop's Fables, and the lessons we are to bring away from Scripture do not snap together like little tiny Legos.

But Old Testament history is *more* than Aesop's Fables, not *less*. We know this on the authority of the Lord Jesus Himself. In His Sermon on the Mount, Jesus gives us an authoritative summary of the entire Old Testament. He says, do unto others as you would have them do unto you (Matt. 7:12)—and He says that this is the law and the prophets. In Christ's reading, the entire Old Testament reduces to an ethical charge. The Golden Rule, learned in many a Sunday School, turns out to actually be the whole point.

In another place, Jesus says that love for God and neighbor sum up the whole Old Testament as well (Matt. 22:40). Now if A=B and B=C, then we can say that A has *something* to do with C. If the two great commandments are the law and the prophets, and the Golden Rule is the law and the prophets, what is the relationship of the two great commandments and the Golden Rule? And has anybody noticed that these dominical summaries of the whole Old Testament are kind of Aesopy? Love God, love your neighbor, and do as you would be done by?

——

There are two significant things going on here. The first is the fact of Christ's willingness to summarize. This is significant because summarization is actually what systematics is. He doesn't say, "Well, it's not that simple . . ." He summarizes the entire Old Testament in words that could fit into one tweet, and room to spare. The second thing is that His summary doesn't mention creation, sin, redemption, the Messiah, or the flow of biblio-redemptive history. I say this fully granting that all these things must be included in what we are summarizing, and that if they are not, we are going to wind up with some sort of anemic and very liberal "brotherhood of man, fatherhood

of God" bromide collection. Moralism as a stand-alone product really is heretical and bad. But it is apparently not bad to
sound moralistic sometimes, like when you are summarizing
the import of the Old Testament.

———

And as they say on TV infomercials, "But wait, there's more."
This information is not just given to us raw, but in more than
one instance we are given a ranking of competing summaries.

"And the scribe said unto him, Well, Master, thou hast said
the truth: for there is one God; and there is none other but
he: And to love him with all the heart, and with all the understanding, and with all the soul, and with all the strength, and
to love his neighbour as himself, is more than all whole burnt
offerings and sacrifices. And when Jesus saw that he answered
discreetly, he said unto him, Thou art not far from the kingdom of God" (Mark 12:32–34a).

Not only does this scribe summarize the Old Testament the
same way Jesus had done, he goes farther and says that this
element of biblical teaching is far to be preferred to religious
ceremony, even when the ceremonies in questions had been
established by God Himself. When he says this, Jesus com-
mends him and says that he is not far from the kingdom.

———

The dogmatism of the Pharisees was not detached from
their covenantal boundary markers. We have all had to deal
with the theological Euclidians who can slice metaphysical
hairs with precision, and when they are done, nobody can
tell any difference. They can take the midges of truth, dissect
them, and tie off their intestines into a little braid, and all while
the rest of us don't even know yet whether or not midges even
have intestines. I mean, think about it.

But the airy-fairy metaphysicians are not a big factor in the biblical text. We have to deal with them, sure enough, reasoning by analogy. But the Pharisees were hair-splitters when it came to ritual, ceremony, practice. When do you wash your hands and feet, and why? What may you eat, and why? When may you eat it? What constitutes Sabbath observance? You may pick up a chair and carry it across the room on the Sabbath, but you may not drag it—for if you drag it, it might break the surface, and that would be *plowing*, and plowing is working on the Sabbath.

And then a man came along, not far from the kingdom, and he said that a monotheistic confession, and loving that God all out, and loving your neighbor as yourself was "more" than "all whole burnt offerings and sacrifices." What was his authority for that systematic summary?

AGAINST DOCTRINE

ONCE UPON A TIME, the king convened a great synod of all the parachurch ministries, and because the times were troublous, they all of them came. WildLife Youth Stampede was there (WYS), the Gospel Blimp Organization (GBO), and IIMEI (If It Moves, Evangelize It) and many others like that—yea, all the staff members of multiple organizations assembled in the Great Hall in their fifties and in their hundreds. But the leadership of all the parachurch ministries fell naturally to the seminaries, the most ancient and respected among these parachurch organizations—the Ur-parachurch, if you will. Some of them were *almost* a hundred years old. And of course, the leadership of the seminaries fell to Bestminster Best. (Unfortunately, because of a scandalous dalliance with obedient and living faith, Bestminster Beast had not been invited.)

Because of this, the spokesman for the *good* Bestminster stood before the great congregation, and spake thus, in the presence of the king.

"Oh, king, as you know, the land is filled with teeming heresies, with the pox, and with many other things of icky countenance. We can do nothing about the latter two (sorry!), but with regard to the first, we beseech you to decree that responsibility for orthodoxy be transferred to us. For we ought to be, as it saith somewhere, the pillar and ground of the truth. The

Church has not exercised leadership in this, and has buried its talent in a napkin. So we dug it up. Can we have it?"

The king, whose name was Assensus, raised his scepter. "Okay," he said. At this the assembly all broke into uproarious laughter—it was just the sort of thing that King Assensus was always saying.

———

J.B. Phillips famously wrote the book *Your God is Too Small*, and I would like to do a little riff off of that: Your doctrine is too small.

Often particular doctrines are set forth in a way that contains enough of the truth to annoy unreasonable people and not enough of the truth to answer the concerns and objections of reasonable people. Let's take three examples—the sovereignty of God, the necessity of the new birth, and the potency of the Incarnation. In each case, when the doctrine is stated in its *small* version, the proposed response is to try to fix the problem by reeling it in, by making it smaller.

When Jonathan Edwards was struggling with the doctrine of God's sovereignty, he found the solution where it actually ought to be. Learn to see God's sovereignty as *bigger* than what we thought. If the sovereign God is simply an omnipotent Zeus, contained together with us inside the universe that is, and he goes around making people do whatever he wants, then the freewillers are right—he is just a bully. Not only are the freewillers right, they are often courageously right. But the problem here is that he is seen as a bully because he is too small, and it is no solution to make him smaller. A Calvinist who has made the same mistake agrees that God is like this but argues a theology of prudence. "Look, just go along with the bully, wouldja?" The Arminian resists this by preferring to see the bully as a kinder, gentler Zeus. The end result of this business is a wimp subbed in for the bully. But the triune God of Scripture is the Creator of all that is, and there actually is a Creator/creature divide. To attribute exhaustive sovereignty to any entity on *this* side of that divide (apart from the humility of the Incarnation) is to ask for, and find, monstrosities in your doctrinal systematics. But the solution is not to be found by dragging the whole thing down to a religion just above tree top level. God dwells in the highest heavens. He does what He pleases, and what He pleases is righteous, holy, and good.

While evangelicals have rightly seen the need to be born again, this too can be seen in a way that is far too small. If the old nature/new nature question is seen as a toggle switch somewhere down in your heart, and at some time in your life you have to pray a prayer that makes God flip that switch, and if you don't do that you are going to go to Hell, this truncated vision of the new birth is going to lead to extreme sectarianism. Evangelicals will become star-bellied Sneetches, and this one isolated experience is the point of their distinction. Lack of regeneration is seen as the switch in *this* position, and you have to have it in *that* position. Now when people see the spiritual pride that often arises from this kind of thing, the temptation is to back away from the evangelical position— well, maybe being born again is not all that it is cracked up to be. Regeneration is seen as too small, and the temptation is to make it smaller. The movement is from a message preached by a narrow hot-gospeler to a broad latitudinarianism that walks away from the little bit of truth that was there.

But when a man is born again, *all of him is.* Regeneration commences at the point of conversion, and this principle of new life then grows and spreads everywhere. Regeneration is not a little toggle switch, but is rather the main power breaker. And after it is flipped, there are still five thousand other switches to find and adjust before this new life spacecraft is ready to fly again. And that is what is happening—we are readying a spacecraft to fly to the heavens. We are not changing a light bulb in the barn. Don't see regeneration as a little thing—there is no way to do that and maintain the necessity of it without that position degenerating into a doctrine that insists that God has no sense of proportion whatever.

When the eternal Word of God became a man, He thereby honored the material world and did so in a very permanent way. This has always been embarrassing to the Hellenistic mind—this has been seen as a doctrine that maintains that God abandoned His spiritual dignity. No, this actually *is* the divine glory. But once the doctrine is stated, if it is limited to the body of Jesus, it remains too small. Incarnational heresies take something that is true as far as it goes, but is still too small, and then try to whittle away at it, making it smaller. The orthodox should not try to hold the line by holding the line, but rather should move on to the other outlandish ramifications of this truth. If Christ is the groom, and the church is His bride, His *body*, what does this mean? We have not understood the Incarnation unless we have come to understand that at some point in the proceedings, the incarnational power that God has placed in the world runs amok. And when it runs amok, this has ramifications for beer, sex, mowing the lawn, planting hedges, gravy, beekeeping, driving on the freeway, and diet soda. And no, those ramifications do not mean pantheism.

Just as grace does not mean antinomianism, but will always provoke charges of antinomianism, so also an understanding of the incarnation as *God's reckless grace to the whole universe* will provoke charges of some heresy or other. And perhaps some will veer off into those heresies, but it cannot be unorthodox to say that our orthodoxy has been too small and that we need a whole lot more of it.

"But as it is written, Eye hath not seen, nor ear heard, neither have entered into the heart of man, the things which God hath prepared for them that love him" (1 Cor. 2:9).

———

When the wrong kind of knowledge puffs up, it accomplishes this by making the puffee think that he is hotter property than he actually is. He knows more, he thinks, than other people around him, and he thinks this because he is grading on a curve. Not only is he grading on a curve, he is doing so erroneously. "Oh, how many knowing men are ignorant."[9]

This is why we shrink our doctrines. The doctrine has to be big enough to impress the yokels, and small enough for a proud theologian to master. The bigness is accomplished by means of jargon, and the smallness is accomplished by means of sin.

———

Paul was familiar with this mentality.

"Not that we are sufficient of ourselves to think any thing as of ourselves; but our sufficiency *is* of God; Who also hath made us able ministers of the new testament; not of the letter, but of the spirit: for the letter killeth, but the spirit giveth life" (2 Cor. 3:5–6).

The letter kills. Paul cannot mean that letters themselves automatically do this, because he is warning of this problem by means of letters. He was not guilty of the problem he was warning against—his ministry was not of letters, but of the Spirit, and we know this because he used letters to tell us.

We make the same mistake with ritual, with doctrine, and with sacraments. We stare *at* instead of looking *through*. So if someone tells you he is a Westminster man, this is not enough

---

9   Thomas Watson, *A Body of Divinity: Contained in Sermons upon the Westminster Assembly's Catechism* (Carlisle, PA: Banner of Truth, 1957), 171.

information. Is he looking at a Westminster mural, or looking through a Westminster window?

———

We are not engaged in a fight to recover biblical language *simpliciter*, but rather in a fight to recover the *right* to use biblical language as necessary. The vocabulary of historic liturgies, systematics, the creeds, and so on are also most necessary, and we should have no interest in ditching them unless absolutely necessary. Our endeavors in this whole area should include fifty years of attempted harmonization. At the same time, what we must reject is such uninspired creedal vocabulary making it impossible to use biblical language (as appropriate) without being called a heretic. I want to be able to use the word *regeneration* in the same way the Synod of Dort did, but I don't want to be told that the usage of that venerable synod outranks Christ's way of talking about life in the Regeneration.

FOR THE NEW BIRTH

Once a great synod of Reformed owls gathered together for a confabulation of their wits, to wit, putting their brains together to solve a problem that had long roiled the world of owley Reformedness. Now, in that last sentence, I must confess that I was sorely tempted to write, "of their wits, to wit, to woo," but that would have been overly clever and arch, if you know what I mean.

At any rate, the owls were assembled in solemn congress to determine if apple trees produced apples because they were apple trees, or if apple tree status was logically distinct, sealed off in a separate ontological category, although everyone acknowledged that apples did keep showing up somehow. One party stoutly maintained that in order to protect the majesty of sovereign grace the apple trees had to be incapable of producing apples and that the apples must be seen as having an independent point of origin. Perhaps the orchard fairies came in the night and hung them there. Or something.

The others, the party in the minority, thought that there had to be a tight organic connection between apple-treeness and the apples.

One of these owls, a large fluffy one named Warmfeather, concluded an impassioned speech on the subject by saying that such a connection was most necessary, although he admitted that he could not explain scientifically or mathematically how this all worked. "On such matters," he quietly said, "we must be intellectually humble. After all, we are only birds with brains the size of a walnut."

Around the great parliament hall, hisses and murmurs went up. "Papist! Pelagian! Rotarian!" taunted one owl, who had a brain the size of a significantly smaller walnut.

Warmfeather rocked back and forth sideways until he recovered both his perch and his composure. But from the far side of the hall, the moderator of this august assembly slowly approached him, and his mitre with the embroidered figure of John Knox on it was slightly askew. Stopping and pausing for dramatic effect, he then coughed up the skeleton of a dead mouse at Warmfeather's feet. Warmfeather looked at it sadly, for in the very small world of Reformed owls, this had only one possible meaning. Warmfeather would never again be a conference speaker at that big oak tree three fields over.

———

It is not possible to make a good omelet with rotten eggs. The new birth deals with the eggs. The church, whenever she is not animated by the regenerating Spirit of God, tries to fix the problematic omelet by means of kitchen upgrades, better recipes, graduate studies for the cooks, and more.

———

The new birth is one thing, but quite a different thing than affirming the absolute necessity of the new birth, which is *another* good thing. But not the same thing.

———

In response to the question, "What more can there be than union with Christ?" the answer would appear to be *permanent* union with Him. And this idea of permanence is one which the Lord certainly talks about. Servants come and go, but sons are forever.

> Then said Jesus to those Jews which believed on him, If ye continue in my word, then are ye my disciples indeed; And ye shall know the truth, and the truth shall make you free. They answered him, We be Abraham's seed, and were never in bondage to any man: how sayest thou, Ye shall be made free? Jesus answered them, Verily, verily, I say unto you, Whosoever committeth sin is the servant of sin. And the servant abideth not in the house for ever: but the Son abideth ever. If the Son therefore shall make you free, ye shall be free indeed. (John 8:31–38)

So then, for those who persevere, how they *subjectively* receive grace is part of what has been *objectively* given. We are to work out our salvation because God is at work in us to will and to do for His good pleasure. My continued subjective positive responses tomorrow must be considered as part of His objective gift to me. We work out what He works in.

In Luke 18, two covenant members go down to the temple to pray. The Pharisee was rigorously orthodox (and *Reformed*) in his formulation. He gave glory to God for all that he had and was (*soli Deo gloria!*). He thanked God that he was not as other men (what do you have that you did not receive as a gift?), and so forth. We see right through this sinful little trick of his, of course, and close our Bibles in order to thank God that we are not like that Pharisee. Sorry, I got sidetracked.

Anyway, the other fellow confessed that he was a sinner and asked God to be merciful to him. God was merciful to him, and so he went home *justified* rather than the other (Luke 18:14). So here is a biblical term to describe what happens to a repentant covenant member who is finally getting his act together. He is justified. Now it might be replied (and should be) that this does not do justice to the other usages of the word *justification* in Scripture. Exactly so, which is why I think we ought not to be trying to come up with biblical phrases or uses only. We should use terms which are *consistent* with Scripture, based on Scripture, and are subordinate to Scripture. We do not pick and choose, but rather harmonize them all. A man can be justified in one sense and not in another. This was the condition of the Pharisee, who went home that day unjustified. The other man had been circumcised and was able to worship in the temple. He was also justified, right? In one sense. But then he went home justified, and so we may assume that he had not arrived that way.

Some might want to say that we have no need to use the word *converted* of such a man because it misleads people. It suggests he never really was in Christ in the first place. But sometimes this is precisely what we need to suggest. Being in Christ is not just *one* thing that is operated by just one on-off switch. The hypocrite is in Christ in one sense, and he is not in Christ in another. Part of our problem is that we want to nail too many things down. Tares are in the wheat field, but they do not partake of ontological wheatness. But when the pietists beat this drum too loudly, they need to be reminded that the fruitless branches in John 15 do partake of ontological branchness.

God is perfect, but He is no perfectionist. He likes to mess with our heads. I suggest we let Him.

———

So when does the moment of regeneration occur anyhow? Fortunately, the answer to that one is simple . . . *who knows? who cares? none of our business!*

Perhaps I should explain.

What I am contending for is an affirmation that such a transformation must occur at *some* point in the lives of those who are going to spend eternity with God. But because every person's story is different, we should not be surprised that the moment of transformation varies, and is known only to God. How could it be otherwise? The Spirit blows as He wishes, and we cannot contain Him.

Some people have a story that makes it pretty clear to them when they were regenerated, give or take five minutes. Convulsive experiences, of a Damascus road type, do happen, and so it is relatively easy to read the time stamp. But, as David Wells points out in his book *Turning to God*, the tendency of some evangelicals has been to make such experiences normative.[10] But there is absolutely no basis for doing this. Why would Paul's experience be normative, as over against Timothy's (2 Tim. 3:15)? As I am fond of saying, you don't have to know what time the sun rose to know that it is up.

But also, as a matter of logic, if I know that it *is* up, then I must also affirm that it rose at *some* point. I don't have to know what moment that was exactly, but I do need to affirm that there was in fact such a moment.

During our Sabbath dinner liturgy, the grandkids are asked a bunch of questions, and among the questions I ask are these—"Do you love God? Are you baptized? Is Jesus in your heart? Will you take the Lord's Supper tomorrow?" Now looking at the sixteen kids who are answering those questions, if someone were to press the question—"But *when* did Jesus come into their hearts?"—the answer is that it is absolutely none of our business.

It could have been in the womb or when they were born or when they were baptized or six weeks, three days, and ten minutes after their baptism. We have no way of knowing that. We can't see hearts, and God does not ask us to conduct

---

10   David F. Wells, *Turning to God* (Grand Rapids: Baker Books, 1989), 29.

our parental or pastoral business as though we could see them. Our business is to support their parents as they bring them up in the nurture and admonition of the Lord, which is exactly what we are doing.

I have said earlier in these discussions that the works of the flesh are manifest (Gal. 5:19). We know that the works of righteousness are also manifest (John 3:21). All this is simply to say that midnight and high noon are not that difficult to tell apart. "Is the sun up?" is an easy question to answer, and we must not get tangled up in the very few moments when it *might* be difficult to answer. My StarWalk app tells me that sunrise this morning was at 4:55 a.m., but what if I had driven east for twenty miles, and then went down in a valley? Supposing I had stood behind a tree?

But knowing *that* the sun is up is easy. Knowing that there had to be a moment when it came up is also easy—which is not the same thing as knowing when, precisely, that moment was.

What I am trying to avoid is a circumstance where folks are sitting around in the middle of the night trying to generate light by making superstitious use of their baptisms, or their decision fifteen years ago in a Child Evangelism bus at the state fair. The dark is what it is.

And what do I mean by superstition? Not to worry—if the sun is up, it is not superstition.

The hardest thing in the world to keep is balance, and this is particularly the case when you are in discussions with folks who think you might not be keeping yours. I have heard it said that some have accounted for my regeneration jag, of which this book is a part, as a ploy to stay in good with John Piper or Mark Driscoll, while others think I am simply returning to my Southern Baptist upbringing. I had tried to run away from home with the other bad Federal Vision boys, but I only made it to the end of the driveway.

However, I am not *returning* to anything. While I am not a Baptist at all (though I like them fine), I *am* an evangelical. I have always been an evangelical, and when this poor lisping, stammering tongue lies silent in the grave, it will be the tongue of a dead evangelical.

But what gives? Over the years, many of my readers have come to understand that I have spent a goodish bit of the energies from my satiric chakras in making fun of evangelicalism. Now this may require some explanation. Evangelicalism can be divided into two broad wings. The first wing houses a sedate wax museum containing the likenesses of such worthies as Jonathan Edwards, A.W. Tozer, and Carl Henry, while the second wing contains the teeming and swollen Barnum & Bailey contingent, not forgetting the tattooed fat lady. In my satiric labors, I have sought to focus my attentions on the latter, and all for the sake of the former.

My father is an old-school evangelical. But he is also one of the most gifted personal evangelists I have ever met. This means that as far back as my memory goes, there is a long line of people getting *saved*, getting converted. And they really were getting converted, lives turned completely around, with all glory and honor going to God. While a number of these folks were heathens, a bunch of them had already been baptized and had their ecclesiastical papers stamped and everything. They still needed Jesus, even though they had been given the Jesus water. In order for them to come to Jesus, they needed an evangelist who saw that they needed to.

Now follow me closely here. At the very same time, because of where I was growing up, and because of the circles we lived in, we were in close proximity to the Barnum & Bailey tents. We could smell the elephants. All the salvation hooey that goes on . . . tell me about it.

One time, a nationally known evangelist came to Moscow, and had a big event at the Student Union on campus. Over eight hundred decisions for Christ were recorded . . . and reported to the Christian community as though they were all in the bank. Now Moscow is a small town, and the Christian community is even smaller. In the months following that event, I was not privileged to meet *one* person out of that eight hundred. Not one. To be fair, I did later meet one Christian who had signed a decision card one of those nights, but he had actually gotten saved later on in some sort of fashion that did not involve the signing of cards.

An odd illustration might help. It was as though I grew up in a wild hare charismatic church, with forehead slappers healing people of popcorn gluttony every Sunday, along with other assorted and zany activities that tried to prove that the Holy Spirit had lost His mind, while at my house my father was quietly healing terminal cancer patients without stretching one syllable words into three syllables words at all. Someone growing up in such circumstances would be somewhat conflicted. When it came to telling stories, like that time the snake basket got knocked over in middle of the revival, he would have the kind of stories to make you wheeze. And yet . . . but . . . all those cancer patients . . .

The excesses of the Great Awakening were very real, and some of the downstream negative consequences of it were equally real. The George Whitefield who published his journal was a very young man and a coxcomb. I agree with Charles Hodge's critique of the whole thing. But that does not mean that the Great Awakening was not from God, or that Whitefield was not greatly used by Him.

———

Here is the thing. Using both terms broadly, revivalists and sacramentalists both make staggering claims for what they are doing. Often the claims are not borne out by what we might call "actual results." The evangelicalism that I am defending is not the hot evangelicalism of Brother Love's Traveling Salvation Show on one more muggy August night. What I am defending is a chastened evangelicalism.

David Brainard ought not to have said that his instructor at Yale had no more grace "than this chair." But let it also be noted that Brainard heartily repented of that comment. Gilbert Tennant ought not to have preached his famous sermon on the dangers of an unconverted ministry (while it *is* dangerous, his language *was* intemperate). But he repented. Jonathan Edwards made his name by cheerleading for the revival, but as time went by his book on the religious affections showed that he was not prepared to accept sin for the sake of protecting his earlier views of the revival.

———

I have already mentioned David Wells's magnificent book on conversion, *Turning to God*. In it you find an evangelical treatment of true conversion that is thoughtful, judicious, biblical, balanced, scholarly . . . and evangelical. That is what I am urging. I'm with him.

———

At the same time, I have not seen the same kind of willingness on the part of sacramentalists to admit that what they are telling us *isn't working*, as measured by those indicators that the New Testament gives us as being inconsistent with inheriting the kingdom of God. What happens is usually special pleading. But when a sacramentalist does acknowledge that some baptized son of the church is a rascal son of Belial, and that something decisive needs to happen to his soul to turn him around, to turn him back to God, that is evangelical enough for me.

———

The New Testament era was born in a hot revival. The movement exploded in a fervor of religious zeal. The accusers at Pentecost thought everybody was drunk, not that everybody was singing Matins. And you find exactly the same pattern in that first generation—a glorious work of the Spirit, inevitable excesses, and judicious leaders of the movement then laying down the marks of a real conversion. The New Testament is jammed with tests to help us distinguish the real ones from the posers.

And the heart of it is this. Real conversions are marked by the *fruit* of the Spirit, not the *gifts* of the Spirit. Regeneration has a tell, and that tell is love. As John Owen noted, the gifts of the Spirit are not the saving grace of the Spirit.[11] And the love we are talking about is not a momentary thing. Love is not a walk around the block, but rather a long-haul trucking trip.

"If someone says, 'I love God,' and hates his brother, *he is a liar*; for the one who does not love his brother whom he has seen, cannot love God whom he has not seen" (1 John 4:20).

So this is how it is possible to be a churchman and an evangelical. Not only is it possible, I believe that rightly understood, the two require each other.

We are told that we are supposed to let the fire of our zeal burn hot—we are supposed to be on the boil (Rom. 12:11).

---

11   John Owen, *The Complete Works of John Owen* (Carlisle, PA: Banner of Truth, 1966), 4.420.

We are also told not to allow this evangelical fire and fervor to run off with us. The spirits of the prophets are subject to the prophets. The structure of the institutional church is necessary, like a fireplace. The flame of true evangelical experience and conviction—a "felt Christ" as the Puritans would say—is the only reason for a fireplace to begin with.

Over the years, as the mansions got bigger and the artisanship that went into the carving of mantelpieces got more cunning, the more time could go by without a fire ever actually being built in that thing. I mean, who wants to fill up such a beautiful hole in the wall with a bunch of ashes?

After a time, others—by which I mean radical charismatics and crazed anabaptists—start setting their fires on the coffee table or the love seat. But at least they knew the room was cold and something should be done about it.

The fire of evangelical conviction, when scripturally governed, cries out for a fireplace to burn in. A well-designed fireplace, put together by biblically minded craftsmen, cries out for a fire to go in it. A fireplace without a fire is cold and dead. A fire without a fireplace is fierce and destructive. Shouldn't we be able to work something out?

All the things I have been writing about the new birth amount to this—without the new birth, you cannot have a church, at least not for very long. Without an established church, you cannot have the new birth. How will they hear without a preacher? With a revival, and many coming to know the Lord, those who love the Lord will seek out fellowship with each other and they will bring their Bibles. And the Bible gives us instructions on how to establish the institution of the church. The Bible brings the fire, and the Bible contains drawings for the fireplace.

There will have to be hard conversations and discussions to allay the nervousness of pretty much everyone. More than one person will say, as Paul did when he came with the famine relief gift to Jerusalem, that this is "the very thing I was eager to do." And more than one person will be annoyed at having to say it. The fireplace men will remind the fire guys that the fireplace is necessary. And the fire guys will make a point of telling the fireplace men that without a fire, the whole thing is pointless. And both sides are right. Everybody has a point.

Evangelical experience is born from the Word, and the Word will cause that experience to seek out the constraints placed upon it by the Word. This need not be a quenching of the Spirit—in the early rounds, it is the Spirit quenching us. A proper bounding of the fire is done in such a way as to enable the fire to burn *hotter*. The identity of each is found in the other.

I said earlier that without the new birth you cannot have the church, and here is the reason. The new birth has a predicate, and that predicate is death—death to sin, death to self, death to striving ambition, and death to lordly pride. If such things do not die, then they will devour the church. If they die (all ecclesiastical variants included), then there will be resurrection and glory.

This principle applies to absolutely everything in our lives, but the one place where we must see it functioning in all its glory has to be the church. There is a Jesus way of losing that gains everything (Luke 9:24; Luke 17:33). There is, of course, a loser way of losing that loses everything. Those same passages tell us the central technique that sinners have for losing, and that is grasping. If you grasp at sermons and sacraments, music and processionals, architecture and solemnity, all of it comes apart in your hands. These things cannot be grasped without breaking them.

We have to hate the church in order to love it properly. "He that loveth his life shall lose it; and he that hateth his life in this world shall keep it unto life eternal" (John 12:25). I am a churchman. I love the church. The church is my life. I love the music, I love the Word, I love the liturgy, I love the Supper, I love the fellowship—I love it all. I recall one time in the midst of the service when my wife leaned over to me and said, "I *love* church." Me too. And that is precisely why we must hate it. We do not hate it the way the devil does, of course not. We hate it the way we are called to hate our mothers (Luke 14:26)— because the church *is* our mother (Gal. 4:26).

There is a way of cursing father or mother that just gets your lamp put out in obscure darkness (Prov. 20:20). The church at Ephesus had fallen from her first love, and was in precisely that danger, that of having her lampstand removed (Rev. 2:4). So that is not the way.

Fortunately, we are not left with contradictory and baffling instructions in this matter. We know how to navigate this with other areas. Do we answer a fool according to his folly or not (Prov. 26:4–5)? Do we honor our parents or hate them (Eph. 6:1–4; Luke 14:26)? Do we give to the hungry or not (Matt. 25:37; 2 Thess. 3:10)?

Scripture does not contradict Scripture, and so our task is to take the whole counsel of God (Acts 20:27), honoring the church in the way the Word describes and showing contempt for the things of the church in the way the Word requires. Such a scriptural contempt might be rendered, depending on the circumstances, toward the sanctuary, the Scriptures, baptisms, ordinations, sermons, seminaries, robes, preaching traditions, communion, choirs, and more. And why?

Not to throw them away in disgust, the way a God-hater would, but rather so that we might have them all in the resurrection. If we die, we shall be raised. And if we are raised, the first thing we will want to do is go to church.

PART TWO

BACKGROUND ASSUMPTIONS

GRACE HAS A BACKBONE

I AM FOND OF SAYING that grace has a backbone, but perhaps it is necessary to explain what is meant by that. The context would be the worrisome trajectories of all those incipient legalists and antinomians out there. The incipient legalists are the ones the incipient antinominans are worried about, and vice versa.

Of course, as things stand right now in the evangelical and Reformed world things are generally copacetic, at least as far as this topic goes. If we lived in a truly confessional age, with great preaching, theological geniuses writing their tomes, and so on, then we would have to worry about the naked Quakers running through Safeway again, and legalistic Anglican bishops cutting off people's thumbs for having broken some stupid rule. But as it is, we are too anemic to get into serious trouble with legalism or antinomianism. We are the bland leading the bland, which provides us with some small measure of imagined safety, at least for a time.

So what is the relationship of the grace of God to the (seemingly unrelated) world of hard moral effort? If the grace of God is in all and through all and beneath us all, then why do we still have to sweat bullets? Are those who sweat bullets abandoning the grace of God? Are those who rejoice in free forgiveness forsaking the demands of discipleship?

My favorite Puritan writer is Thomas Watson, and one of his book is *Heaven Taken by Storm*, his exposition of Matthew 11:12.[12] Throughout the book Watson seems to regard the whole grace/works thing with a serene and admirable above-it-all-ness. He will say, on the one hand, that while Christ bled, *you* must sweat. But on the other hand, he says, "Though we shall not obtain the kingdom *without* violence, yet it shall also not be obtained *for* our violence."

I am reminded of a comment that Spurgeon once made when asked how he reconciled divine sovereignty with human responsibility. He replied that he did not even try—he never sought to reconcile friends. If we think about it rightly, from the vantage of those jealous for moral probity, we will never try to reconcile grace with works—that would be like trying to reconcile an apple tree with its apples. And, if we think about it rightly, from the vantage of those jealous for the wildness of grace, we will never try to reconcile grace with merit, for the two are mortal enemies and cannot be reconciled.

But those who insist that apple trees must always produce apples will make the friends of free grace nervous, not because they have anything against apples, but rather because they know the human propensity for manufacturing shiny plastic apples, with the little hooks that make it easy to hang them, like so many Christmas tree ornaments, on our doctrinal and liturgical bramble bushes. But on the other hand, those who insist that true grace always messes up the categories of the ecclesiastical fussers make the friends of true moral order nervous—because there are, after all, numerous warnings (from people like Jesus and Paul, who *should* have a place in these particular discussions, after all) about those who "live this

---

12   Thomas Watson, *The Christian Soldier or Heaven Taken by Storm: Showing the Holy Violence a Christian is to Put Forth in the Pursuit after Glory* (Whitefish, MT: Kessinger Publishing, 2010).

way" not inheriting the kingdom. Kind of cold, according to some people, but the wedding banquet is the kind of event you *can* get thrown out of.

So what is the relationship of grace to hard, moral effort? Well, hard, moral effort *is* a grace. It is not every grace, but it is a true grace. It is a gift of God, lest any should boast. We are God's workmanship, created in Christ Jesus to do good works, and this is a description of someone being saved by grace through faith, and not by works (Eph. 2:8–10).

This is all summed up in another glorious passage as well— "work out your own salvation with fear and trembling. For it is God which worketh in you both to will and to do of his good pleasure" (Phil. 2:12–13). We are called to work out what God works in, *and absolutely nothing else.* If we don't work out that salvation (as evidenced by the fruit of it), then that is clear evidence that God is not working anything in.

If we work out some pressboard imitation (a salvation that has the look of real wood!), then that shows that God is not working anything in there either. Moralism is just a three-dollar flashlight to light the pathway to Hell. And of course, if we are guilty of the opposite error, if our lives are manifesting a lineup of dirty deeds done dirt cheap, the only real sin we are avoiding is that of hypocrisy. Overt immorality is the fifty-dollar flashlight.

This is why we need a little more of "in Him we live and move and have our being." Actually, we need a *lot* more of it. The answer to the grace/works dilemma is high octane Calvinism, and by this, I don't mean the formulaic kind. If God is the one Paul preached—the one of whom it can be said "of him, and through him, and to him, are all things"—then where in the universe are you going to hide your damned dinky merit? If He is Almighty God, and He starts to transform your tawdry little life into something resembling Jesus, who are you to tell Him that He is now wavering on the brink of dangerous legalisms?

By the way, my use of *damned* a few lines up was not frivolous swearing. I meant damned merit. And no, I don't think I am C.S. Lewis.

The bottom line is that we cannot balance our notions of grace with works or our notions of works with grace. We need to get off that particular teeter-totter. We have to balance absolutely everything in our lives with God Himself, who is the font of everlasting grace—real grace. Real grace is the context of everything. If we preach the supremacy of God in Christ, and the absolute lordship of that bleeding Christ, and the efficacious work of the Spirit in us who raised Jesus from the dead, then a number of other things will resolve themselves in a multitude of wonderful ways. Those wonderful ways will be seen by a watching world as something they will call good works. We can call them that too, if we want, as Paul makes free to do in Titus. And when unbelievers ask us where these works come from, we need to chuckle and say, "Where everything does. From Jesus, man."

In Jesus, we are the new humanity. Is Jesus grace or works? Jesus lives in the garden of God's everlasting favor, and we are in Him. In Christ, there are no prohibited trees. Outside Him, they are *all* prohibited. That means there is only one real question to answer, and it does not involve any grace-works ratios. The question is more basic than that, and has to do with the new birth.

Many theological problems are created by turning certain issues into *theological* problems. As Yogi Berra might have said.

Personal regeneration is an important topic in theology, but it is also a very practical issue. But this is only a theological problem because we are dealing with it on the blackboard, as a abstract problem involving *categories*. But personal regeneration is *personal*, and the most important thing about it is not its placement in the right category. *You* must be born again.

Here is how we stumble. Take a basic truism of Reformed theology—the doctrine of the antithesis. While doing this, never forget that truisms are true, but also guard against using the abstracted truth as a shield to guard against the actual truth. And in this case, here is how it is frequently done.

"I am guarding the antithesis," a man might solemnly say, as he haggles over one of his pet doctrines. But what makes this work? It is the assumption that "the antithesis" is between righteousness and unrighteousness, abstractly considered. And since his pet doctrine is on the side of righteousness, in the same column on the blackboard, in fact, it must be a faithful representation of the "antithesis."

But the antithesis is not a theological form of A and not A. It is not the contrast between right and wrong. It is not between righteousness and unrighteousness. The antithesis divides *people*—the seed of the woman and the seed of the serpent. We are talking about billions of personal names—mothers, fathers, wives, husbands, sons and daughters.

The antithesis is not about abstracted categories at all. Upholding and defending the antithesis means doing whatever we can to keep a clear distinction between those *people* who walk in the light and those *people* who, hating their brother, continue to walk in darkness.

This is where the doctrine of personal regeneration comes in. I don't care what you call it—transformation, conversion to God, effectual call, being born again to God—but this reality is the only thing that will enable us to make faithful sense of the secular and ecclesiastical worlds around us.

Now there are two basic ways to mess this up. One is to *deny* the antithesis, which is the route of saccharine do-gooders, weepy universalists, chagrined hand-wringers, and other exegetical bed-wetters. The indivisibility of the human race (their godhead) is assumed, declared, preached, and exalted. This dogma is then ferociously applied to any who might call it into question. So this "we are the world" position is forced to acknowledge that the only divisible segment of the human race consists of those Christians who blasphemously posit the divisibility of the human race. Since this sets up a clear absurdity that their secular apologists cannot solve, these angular and uncooperative Christians have to be quickly shouted down and then frogmarched off for their (tax-supported) Inclusivity Training Camp. This accounts for why the tolerant and inclusive can become so savage so quickly.

The other error is to affirm but then to misplace the antithesis. Some make the antithesis personal, which is good, but they also make it tribal or racial. This was the error of the Judaizers in the first century, and it is the error of various racialists today. But others, in defense of orthodoxy, misplace the antithesis by making it a division of abstract categories. But it is nothing of the kind. It is the division between those people who are the seed of the woman and those people who are the seed of the serpent. These two groups of *people* have antipathy settled between them (by the decree of God), and nothing whatever can be done to dissolve that antipathy in various humanistic or ecumenical solvents.

So here is the problem, and this is why the doctrine of the absolute necessity of the new birth is so important. The fundamental antithesis is between those who are their way to Heaven and those who are on their way to Hell. We are invited (in numerous places in the Scriptures) to consider our earthly lives in the light of our ultimate destinations. The rich fool is *not* encouraged to say or think, "Well, I know I am lost for all eternity, but for a while there I sure had enough money to build some bigger barns!" This vantage of eternity (and only this) gives us genuine perspective on our lives. We may affirm other doctrinal truths alongside this one, but we may never mute or diminish the absolute necessity of the new birth for every son or daughter of Adam. If we lose that battle, we lose the war.

None of this is being said to take away from the importance of the church, which is the body of Christ. The eschatological church is identical to the company of the elect, and on that great day, there will be no confusion or blurring of our categories at all. But until then, in the mess of history, the historical church contains wheat and tares, sheep and pigs, brothers and false brothers. This means that if we allow historical categories to trump eschatological ones, we will wind up offended by the historical antipathy that God settled between the seed of the woman (in history) and the seed of the serpent (in history). And if we are offended at what God has done in this, we will soon be stumbled and offended by what He has done elsewhere. If we don't repent of this, we will not succeed in removing the antithesis which so offends us—but we might manage to turn coat.

At the same time, those who want to affirm the central importance of regeneration, but who also want to assert that they have the power to peer into hearts and determine who around here is *really* born again and who not, are preserving an important truth (the need for personal regeneration), but they are paying far too high a price for it. That price is that they have also introduced the very dangerous sectarian (and—sorry everybody!—baptistic) impulse into the life of the church. We, the Pure and Lovely, consist of "thee and me, and I have my doubts about thee."

But those who want to affirm the central importance of the church in history, but who also want to act as though if you are "baptized, it's all good," are just begging for marginal Christianity to take root everywhere. And marginal Christianity is always tare-Christianity, not wheat-Christianity. These folks are also paying too high a price for the raggedy piece of the truth that they manage to preserve.

And so this is why we preach Christ. This is why we preach Christ crucified. This is why we call all men to be converted to God, so that they might live faithful and gracious lives—a gift from the hand of God. This is why we are rightly called evangelicals. Christ died, was buried, and rose again on the third day so that we could walk in newness of life.

The unregenerate heart has only two motions it can make—trying to climb to God on its own or trying to run away from God.

The unregenerate heart can understand the holiness of God and flee from Him, or misunderstand it and try to attain to it on its own. Only the converted heart can see the holiness as gladness, and the gladness as righteousness, and the righteousness as glory, and love all of it. As John Piper has argued concerning 1 Timothy 1:11, we have to have our eyes opened so that we see the gospel of the glory of the gladness of God. Would this really resolve all our issues about antinomianism and legalism? Taste and see.

Historic evangelicalism (rightly understood) is therefore not one more sectarian option among many. It is the lived experience of potent grace that actually resolves many of these sectarian conflicts and debates. But it only resolves them when the Spirit is actually moving—codified and abstracted evangelicalism resolves nothing, and a great sermon preached seventy-five years ago, pinned up carefully as a dusty parchment in a museum display case, doesn't have the same effect it once did. And the empty display case right next to that one, the case containing the Spirit who moves just as He wills, doesn't attract the visitors it once did. Whenever we open up that display case, it just smells kind of musty.

Outside the museum, the real litmus test, if I may be so bold, is to manage to be accused *simultaneously* of antinomianism and legalism. When you have gotten to the point where any stick is good enough to beat you with, then you really have something. This is like what one Puritan called the bracing experience of "living in the high mountain air of public calumny." The legalists think you are a libertine, and the libertines think you are a fusser, and they all say so in loud voices. That's the ticket.

For many among the contemporary Reformed, a legalist is someone who loves Jesus more than they do, and an antinomian is one who appears to enjoy loving Jesus like that. And if this ever happens on a large scale, it will be a great revival and reformation, recognized as such by the museum curators of the future.

THAT OLD DEVIL DUALISM

Some might want to argue that I am only saying this as a preacher, but I still want to maintain that sin is bad. But what kind of bad? We often know *that* something is bad, but don't spend enough time thinking about why it is bad. In our circles, we spend a lot of time attacking dualism, which is certainly a noble enterprise, but dualism is a sneaky devil, and so we have to guard against dualism creeping into our attacks on it.

First, we have to set aside the childish error of thinking that dualism is anything that "comes in twos." For example, heaven and earth are not dualism, and neither are sun and moon, or land and sea, male and female, heart and head, or body and soul. God loves pairs, and loving pairs is not dualism.

Dualism separates two things that ought to exist in harmony. To acknowledge the existence of two distinct things that ought to be in harmony is not dualism.

Take the simple scriptural example, one that illustrates how men can miss Heaven by eighteen inches—the distance between the heart and the head. How could this be dualism? "Wherefore the Lord said, Forasmuch as this people draw near me with their mouth, And with their lips do honour me, But have removed their heart far from me, And their fear toward me is taught by the precept of men" (Isa. 29:13). The outward profession, what is said by the lips, what is coming out of the head, is one thing, and what is going on in the heart is quite another. There it is, dualism.

But in these mixed up times, we more often find that the person who dares to maintain the mere existent reality of an "inner" and "outer" man is the one accused of dualism, and the one who worships God on Sunday and is a porn freak on Tuesday is the one who makes the accusation.

The Bible repeatedly warns us about the danger posed by our dualistic deceptions, the danger created by ignoring what Scripture tells us about lining up our inner and outer lives. Sin separated them, and it is the work of the Spirit to harmonize them again. But it not harmonization to suppose that they are already fine because "you are not dualistic," and the distinction between inner and outer man is meaningless to you. If you are still sinning, yes, you are dualistic—to that extent and in that degree.

So the point is not that dualism is sin. It is the other way around. For those who have ears to hear it, the point is that all sin is dualism. And you cannot get sin to vanish like it was a vampire and your anti-dualism mantra were the sign of the cross at the break of day.

When God judges the heart, He does so because sinners love the kind of dualism that gives their sin a place to hide. "You are near in their mouth but far from their mind" (Jer. 12:2b, NKJV).

But when someone is unconverted, that condition is not a mystic invisibility, seen only by God. No, it comes out in his life, in his ways. This is why Paul says that the works of the flesh are *manifest*. "I, the Lord, search the heart, I test the mind, even to give every man according to his ways, according to the fruit of his doings" (Jer. 17:10, NKJV).

In our sin, we want to keep inside and outside distinct, so that we can "manage" them, so we can run our simplistic little inventory systems. But in the judgment, the Lord treats the whole thing as an integrated unit. The sinner wants to plead that while he may have sin in his heart, at least he says the Creed and tithes (sometimes). Christ must be here somewhere. The Lord sees the sin in the heart, and the Creed, and the money, and the constant anger toward family, and the porn, and the envious snark, and no Christ anywhere. And when Christ is not present, blessing, His absence is manifest.

So there is a stark difference between light and darkness in the soul of a man. When a person is converted, and I mean really *converted*, there is a transformation that is palpable. It is all of grace, and so there is no sense in anyone taking pride in it, but it really happens in real time to real people.

One of the arguments against this is that we are all of us "bad Christians," and when professing Christians sin, however grievously, they should just be pointed to Christ—Christ in the Word, Christ in their baptism, Christ in the Supper. This is a move that is reluctant to draw a foundational dividing line between wicked men and good men within the boundaries of the covenant.

There is actually something attractive about this, and one of the reasons is the element of truth to it. If God were to mark iniquities, who could stand (Ps. 130:3)? If Bildad is to be believed, the Lord sees faults in the stars (Job 25:5), and so how much more with us? No man is blameless, no man is righteous, and all need salvation by Christ. In this sense, we are all bad Christians.

But we still have to be careful. This must not be taken in a way that flattens moral categories for us or in us, the moral categories we need in order to function within the body in an obedient way. For example, how can we vote for elders if no man can be *blameless* (1 Tim. 3:2)?

"Do all things without murmurings and disputings: That ye may be blameless and harmless, the sons of God, without rebuke, in the midst of a crooked and perverse nation, among whom ye shine as lights in the world" (Phil. 2:14–15).

But in order for the light to *shine*, someone has to flip the switch.

God effects and expects a moral distinction between His people and the world. And when the world starts to flood into the church (in the form of unconverted professors of faith), this line starts to blur. The church is in the world the way a ship is in the ocean, and that is the way it should be. But bad things start happening when the ocean gets into the ship.

Peter tells Simon Magus—a baptized believer, remember— that he is still in bondage. "Repent therefore of this thy wickedness, and pray God, if perhaps the thought of thine heart may be forgiven thee. For I perceive that thou art in the gall of bitterness, and in the bond of iniquity" (Acts 8:22–23).

Why didn't Peter tell Simon that we are all bad Christians? Compared to the infinite holiness of God, that would have been quite correct, but also quite beside the point. Scripture teaches us that there is a vertical comparison which is impossible to survive unless we are clothed in the obedience of Jesus Christ. Without the imputed righteousness of Jesus, we are all lost. But the Bible also shows us how to make horizontal comparisons (without ever forgetting the humility we should have learned at the point of the vertical comparison). Otherwise, there would be no way to vote for elders, choose a spouse, hire an accountant, chase a thief out of your shop, or remonstrate with anyone about anything. Job was a righteous man, one who stopped his mouth, abashed, before the holiness of the God who spoke to him from the whirlwind. That didn't keep him from being *right* in his dispute with his three counselors.

The regeneration that happens in conversion is a fundamental change, but not an exhaustive one. After Eustace was transformed from his dragon shape, no one could be mistaken about the fact that he had been undragoned. It was a fundamental and obvious change. But it was not complete and final. "To be strictly accurate, he began to be a different boy. He had relapses. There will still many days when he could be very tiresome. But most of those I shall not notice. The cure had begun."[13] When we sin, we are all of us dealing with the dragon in our hearts. But there is a difference between that and being a dragon—even a baptized dragon.

With all this noted, we can see why we need a word to describe the heart transformation that occurs in everyone who goes to heaven. And we need a word to describe the imputation of Christ's righteousness to the sinner. We already have stipulated theological definitions for *regeneration* and *justification*. Why change them? Some might want a more strictly exegetical name or words for these realities. I am not necessarily against this, but the disadvantage that a biblical name has when it is being used in a precise, theological way is that the need for consistency and precision can then displace the broader (and more gloriously sloppy) connotations that are usually found in any biblical usage. How does the Bible use *hypostasis*? Does anyone really care anymore?

So we have a visible word, regeneration, for an invisible reality. If we take all this at face value will we be tempted to start trying to read hearts? Jesus teaches us that the moment of regeneration is beyond our power to manipulate (John 3:8), but He also teaches, equally clearly, that the effects of regeneration are entirely visible (John 3:8).

The theological problem is this. At the Last Day, everything will be completely visible to everybody. At the moment of baptism, the condition of the recipient's heart is invisible to us, known only to God—and this is true whether or not we are talking about infant baptism or a profession of faith by an adult.

Since we know that some make it through the laver of regeneration (Titus 3:5) unregenerate—because not all covenant members are elect—the question can be posed this way.

---

13 C.S. Lewis, *The Voyage of the* Dawn Treader (New York: HarperCollins, 1952), 112.

At the moment of baptism, when an unregenerate person is faking his way into the covenant community, can we tell the difference between a sincere, regenerate, elect convert and an insincere, unregenerate, and reprobate one?

Usually, no. Sometimes we can, as when a scoffer tells his carousing friends that he is going to join the church so he can get a cute wife and that he will be back among them soon enough. People join churches for all kinds of reasons that are in equal parts false *and* visible. Some want to sell insurance, while others want to keep peace in the family. And there are always the cute girls.

By visible, I mean visible in principle to a creaturely eye, not visible to everybody equally.

And so usually, no. The elders are not given a spiritual MRI of every convert's soul. We take professions of faith charitably, and we do the same with the covenant vows that parents make when they bring their children to be baptized.

So if someone asks whether at *that* moment, at the moment of baptism, there is any difference between the sincere and insincere recipient, a question can come back this way. From which vantage? From the standpoint of the decrees? We can't know those, and shouldn't try (Deut. 29:29). From the standpoint of the Last Day? We aren't there yet. But this binary choice is far too simple and doesn't come close to accounting for all the biblical data. It is not the case that we have to choose between cracking open the decrees of God at the font on the one hand, and waiting for the last trump on the other.

Three examples of different kinds of soul-assessment come immediately to mind, and I have no doubt there are others. Remember, the apostle Paul says that the works of the flesh are *manifest* (Gal. 5:19), and those who do such manifest things will not inherit the kingdom of God (Gal. 5:21). And it is manifest that they will not inherit the kingdom of God.

First, the Bible teaches us that the credibility of the profession of others may be called into question in the heat of lawful, polemical controversy. In the midst of controversy, the apostle Paul declared that those who wanted to require circumcision of the Gentiles were "false brothers" (Gal. 2:4). He says that they were "dogs," "evil workers," "mutilators of the flesh" (Phil. 3:2). He doesn't go so far as to call them Episcopalian bishops, but he certainly comes close.

Second, the Scriptures teach us that the church may, after careful thought and investigation, decide that a baptized person should be treated as a heathen tax collector (Matt. 18:17). This happens after that person's baptism, and long before the Last Day. Such a determination can be done right. In order to be faithful to Scripture, it must be done right. This determination is being made from within history, and not from the vantage of the decrees or the front seats on the balcony of the Eschaton.

And the third situation might be called that of pastoral admonition. Let's look again at Peter's rebuke of Simon Magus, which occurred a very short time after his baptism: "Thy money perish with thee, because thou hast thought that the gift of God may be purchased with money. Thou hast neither part nor lot in this matter: for thy heart is not right in the sight of God. Repent therefore of this thy wickedness, and pray God, if perhaps the thought of thine heart may be forgiven thee. For I perceive that thou art in the gall of bitterness, and in the bond of iniquity" (Acts 8:20–23).

Peter looked at the hands and wallet of Simon Magus and made a statement about the bondage his *heart* was in.

Now the fact that all three of these situations found in Scripture can and have been wrongfully applied does not make their correct application impossible. People have been called false brothers for the flimsiest of reasons—having had it done to me repeatedly, I certainly don't want to promote that. But the abuse does not negate the use. *Abusus non tollit usus.* People have been excommunicated for parking in the spot reserved for the pastor's wife. Okay, so quit doing that to everybody. And hubristic sectarian pastors have pronounced on the obvious lack of regeneration displayed by someone who failed to dot all five i's in "denominational distinctives." That can't be good.

But, with all this said, to adopt a simple binary scheme between baptism and the last day is really to close the door on effective pastoral care and the cure of souls. I have noticed a tendency among some, in the name of handling the covenant objectively, to treat the manifest sins of some as though the import of those sins were not equally manifest. But I fear that this will eventually amount to sacrificing biblical language on the altar of systematics—which is precisely the thing we were trying to get away from.

PART THREE

THE FATHER PRINCIPLE

LIFE IN THE REGENERATION

IF WE HEAR A WORD ENOUGH, we *think* we know what it means. We live in a Christian subculture that has strongly emphasized the need to be born again. Without denying this need for regeneration at all, we still have to place the reality of this in a biblical context, lest we turn it into something entirely unbiblical—which we have been in great danger of doing.

> Who is the image of the invisible God, the firstborn of every creature: For by him were all things created, that are in heaven, and that are in earth, visible and invisible, whether they be thrones, or dominions, or principalities, or powers: all things were created by him, and for him: And he is before all things, and by him all things consist. And he is the head of the body, the church: who is the beginning, the firstborn from the dead; that in all things he might have the preeminence . . . (Col. 1:12–22)

This is a particularly rich text, but in order to see it rightly we first have to put away an unbiblical set of assumptions. Whenever we hear the word *regeneration*, we think of individuals getting saved, or not. This is *entailed* by the biblical concept of regeneration, and required by it, but if we begin and end here, we will have a gross distortion of the Bible's teaching. The gospel is not limited to the salvation of atomistic individuals.

The common assumption is that God drops a rope from heaven, and then the theological debates begin. Pelagians want to shinny up the rope, Arminians want to hang on while

God pulls, Calvinists say that God ties the rope to us with one of *His* knots, and some of our more severe brethren think He ties it around our necks before He hauls us up. Within the constraints of *this* debate, the Calvinists are quite right. But note that something is still wrong with the entire picture. The illustration itself limits us in ways the Bible does not. Within those constraints, the Calvinists are correct, but there is more going on outside those constraints.

We need to recover an understanding of the glory of the regeneration, and we begin by looking at what the word means, and then at how the Bible applies it. Regeneration refers to rebirth after death. With this in mind, what do we learn from Scripture about regeneration?

First, *Jesus was born again.* In our text above, we learn that Jesus was the firstborn from the dead (Col. 1:18). Our father Adam plunged us into a condition of death. Jesus entered into that Adamic death, and was born again from that death. The apostle Paul quotes the second Psalm ("Thou art my Son, this day have I *begotten* thee") and applies it to the resurrection (Acts 13:33). Because Jesus was born again from the dead, everything else can be born again from the dead. And this is what we see. Unless Jesus was born again from the dead, no one else could be born again from the dead. Unless Jesus was raised from the dead, we are all still in our sins, which is the same thing as still being in our death.

Second, *the entire cosmos was born again.* Our text again says that Jesus was the firstborn of every creature. This principle of new life was placed at the heart of the cosmic order and began to work its way out. "And Jesus said unto them, Verily I say unto you, That ye which have followed me, *in the regeneration* when the Son of man shall sit in the throne of his glory, ye also shall sit upon twelve thrones, judging the twelve tribes of Israel" (Matt. 19:28). The creation longs for the culmination of this glorious process (Rom. 8:22). The regeneration referred to here is the regeneration of heaven and earth, which would not have been possible apart from the resurrection—the engine of this cosmic regeneration.

Third, *Israel was born again*. In his famous conversation with Nicodemus, Jesus pressed this particular point. You (*all*) must be born again (John 3:7). You are a teacher of *Israel*, and you don't know this? This is what Ezekiel so wonderfully predicted for Israel (Ezek. 36:25–28; 37:11). Israel was born again, and so we are now members of the new Israel, the Christian church. The valley of dry bones came to life, and all Israel stood to its feet.

And finally, *John Smith was born again*. But we must place this in its right context. Jesus said "a man" must be born again if he is to see the kingdom of heaven (John 3:3, 5). Our passage in Colossians descends from the cosmic heights to tell the Colossian Christians how it was applied to them. After Christ accomplished the cosmic new birth (v. 20), He brings this new life to those who had been alienated through sin (v. 21). It is the same here. Without the resurrection, without the transformation of the heavens and earth, without the reconstitution of the new Israel, there is no such thing as individual regeneration. We do not say that corporate regeneration makes individual regeneration superfluous, but rather we say that corporate and cosmic regeneration makes individual regeneration both *possible* and *mandatory*. The world has been reconciled to God through Christ. Therefore, Paul presses the point. Be therefore reconciled.

Compare this to getting wet. What difference does it make *how* you get wet? Just so long as you do? The problem here has to do with autonomous man's desire to control and manage this thing. But Christ has remade the world, and we cannot control what He is doing. It makes a difference whether you got wet because someone spritzed a little moisture in your face or you got wet because the tsunami hit the beach. The issue of control is *always* the issue, really. One of the central features of Christ's teaching on regeneration is ignored or twisted by us, because we cannot handle the fact that God has never been domesticated by man. The wind blows where it wants, Jesus taught us (John 3:8). Some people try to bottle the wind—and tell others how to be born again. Others ignore this by pretending that Jesus must be talking about gentle zephyrs, playing quietly among the flowers. But perhaps He wanted us to think about a typhoon.

If our thinking about regeneration begins and ends with the individual, we will drastically misunderstand the nature of God's work in the world. If it never gets down to the individual level, the confusion is just as bad. When a man is summoned by an evangelist to the new birth, he is not being summoned into a private chamber, where mysterious things happen to him as an individual. Rather, the evangelist declares that Jesus has been born again from the dead. Because Jesus has been born again from the dead, He is the Lord over all creation, and all creation, the heavens and the earth, rejoice in having been made new. God has also raised Israel from the dead so that a new Israel might be God's nation in this new creation. The unregenerate individual is told that everything around him has been transformed and that he might as well come along quietly. Behold, the Lord Jesus, the Savior of the *world.*

The new life in Jesus Christ is a reality in the heart of each individual genuinely converted to God. But this new life has come to pass in a new world, a world or age that Jesus called the Regeneration (Matt. 19:2).

So as we talk about what it means to be "born again," we have to preserve the scriptural pattern and order. First, as the cornerstone of *all* doctrines of regeneration, Jesus was born again from the dead (Col. 1:18). Because of Christ's birth from among the dead, the whole created order was made new in Him. We have a new heaven and a new earth because of Him. He is the firstborn of all creation (Col. 1:15). Jesus was raised from the dead *for us*, so that He might be the first born among many brethren (Rom. 8:29). In doing this for us, Christ accomplished the resurrection of Israel (Ezek. 37:1–14), which is why Nicodemus, a teacher in this Israel, should have known what Christ was talking about (John 3:7). You *all* must be born again. But this national regeneration carries individuals with it. *A man* must be born again to see the kingdom of God (John 3:3, 5)

It should not surprise us to find pockets of "unregeneration" in this world made new. The yeast works through the loaf gradually. But the yeast is alive, and brings life to the whole. Thus we find creatures who hate the new creation around them. Thus we find baptized covenant members who inexplicably hate the church of the firstborn that claims them by baptism. No matter. Let God be true, and every man a liar—for the time being.

ONE VAST BONEYARD

CHRIST DIED FOR THE WORLD, and if we are to follow the Apostle Paul's argument, this means that we have an obligation to see that world differently. We are not to see the world as saved after it is saved in fact. We are called to see the world as saved in principle, beforehand, in the reality of Christ's death and resurrection. We should not see the world as saved when our eyes tell us it is all right for us to believe. Who hopes for what he already has? The world will be saved because we see Christ crucified and risen, and so we declare to the world what that means. What is it that overcomes the world? Is it not our faith?

The apostle tells us that how we see non-Christians is directly related to how we see Jesus (2 Cor. 5:16). We like to think that a high Christology and a low cosmology go together, but they do not. We like to think that a high Christology and a low anthropology go together, but they do not. New Age mystics and distorters notwithstanding, we worship a cosmic Christ. Externalists notwithstanding, we worship a personal, heartfelt Jesus.

"For we commend not ourselves again unto you, but give you occasion to glory on our behalf, that ye may have somewhat to answer them which glory in appearance, and not in heart" (2 Cor. 5:12).

We are constrained by the love of Christ, knowing that His was the kind of death that encompasses. If one died for all, then all for whom He died have also died. He died for them in their sins so that they might live for Him outside of their sins. He died and rose. How can *anything* be the same anymore?

Believing this to be the case, we are not permitted to understand any man "after the flesh." There is a way of understanding humanity that does not take into account what Jesus did on the cross and what He accomplished when He rose from the grave. That way of understanding humanity may call itself "realistic," but how is it realistic to ignore the new creation? That way of understanding may point to the orthodox doctrine of total depravity (which *is* the orthodox and biblical doctrine), but how is it that we have come to believe that total depravity has more power to hold down Jesus than the stone tomb did? The fact that Jesus was buried in a stone tomb is a biblical doctrine also, *but that was not the end of the story.*

Yes, unregenerate mankind is totally depraved. Yes, it is true that we cannot autonomously contribute in any way to our own salvation. Yes, it is true that we were dead in our trespasses and sins. But let us never preach the doctrine of total depravity without also declaring there has been a great earthquake, and that an angel of the Lord has rolled away the stone in front of that imposing doctrine.

"Wherefore henceforth know we no man after the flesh: yea, though we have known Christ after the flesh, yet now henceforth know we him no more" (2 Cor. 5:16).

This is crazy talk, I know. But it is also biblical talk. This whole world, since the sin of Adam, has been nothing but one, vast, pole-to-pole boneyard. Whatever would Jesus do in a world like that? What could He possibly do that could transform a world like that? The gospel reply is that *He could come back from the dead in it.*

Billions of sinners, dead in their sins. Son of man, shall these bones live? Ah, sovereign Lord, you know. Son of man, prophesy to the bones. But Lord, bones can't hear. Son of man, prophesy to the bones. But Lord, they are not paying any attention. They have ear holes, but no ear drums. Son of man, prophesy to the bones. But Lord, that's not how I learned to do it in seminary. Son of man, prophesy to the bones. But Lord . . . but Lord . . .

To see men after the flesh is to see nothing but the bones.

"Therefore if any man be in Christ, he is a new creature: old things are passed away; behold, all things are become new" (2 Cor. 5:17).

The newness does not follow the gospel result, but precedes it. The newness calls new life into being. The gospel is not vindicated by conversions; conversions are vindicated and made possible by their participation in the great cosmic conversion. We do not invite Jesus into our lives—down here in the boneyard. Jesus invites us into His life, and the whole world is invited.

"And all things are of God, who hath reconciled us to himself by Jesus Christ, and hath given to us the ministry of reconciliation; To wit, that God was in Christ, reconciling the world unto himself, not imputing their trespasses unto them; and hath committed unto us the word of reconciliation. Now then we are ambassadors for Christ, as though God did beseech you by us: we pray you in Christ's stead, be ye reconciled to God" (2 Cor. 5:18–20).

The ministry of reconciliation is based on the fact of the cosmic reconciliation. People reconciling with God does not create the ministry of reconciliation. The ministry of reconciliation brings the fact to those who have already been reconciled and yet still need to be reconciled. What is so hard about building on the foundation that God has established? You have been reconciled; therefore, be reconciled.

Some may object that this dilutes the truth of definite atonement. Not in the slightest. All who were purchased for eternal salvation by Christ will in fact be eternally saved. Those who were not so purchased will not be. The point here is not that

Christ died indiscriminately for every last man, whether elect or damned. The point is that Christ died for the *world*, and those who are excluded from Christ are therefore excluded from that world—they are cast into the outer darkness. To be saved is to be saved into the new humanity. It is to be saved *into the world*.

But it further means that definite atonement is not synonymous with "tiny atonement." The reality of definite atonement is seen in the specific numbers allotted to each tribe—twelve thousand from each tribe, no more, no less. The majestic extent of definite atonement is seen when John turned and looked. What did he see? He saw *a multitude that no man can number.* How many will be saved? We can't count that high. Look at the stars, Abraham. Use the Hubble telescope, Abraham. So shall your descendants be.

How will these things happen? What will bring it to pass? The glorious message of a glorious substitution will be declared and presented to every living creature. What shall we tell them? We should give them the message we we were told to give to them. We should prophesy to the bones.

"For he hath made him to be sin for us, who knew no sin; that we might be made the righteousness of God in him" (2 Cor. 5:21).

In John 8, Jesus has a remarkable interaction with the Jewish leaders, an interaction that teaches us what it means to be an evangelical indeed.

Jesus had collided with these men, and they did not grasp what He was talking about. They did not grasp it because they did not know the Father. They did not get it because He was from above and they were from below—and unless you are born from above, you cannot even see the kingdom. It is clear in this interaction that for Jesus being "from below" did not mean being a creature, but rather meant being the kind of person who dies in his sins. He says they will die in their sin (v. 21). He says they are from below (v. 23). He says again they will die in their sin (v. 24). This is moral blindness and stupidity; it is not creaturely limitation or finitude.

The thing that had them confused was that their papers were all in order. They were born of Abraham, and Abraham was from above, darn it. Abraham was from God, Moses was from God too, the Torah was from God, and whatever could Jesus be talking about? They had taken a heavenly gift, dragged it down *below* where they were, laid it sideways on the ground so they could stand on it in order to boast.

Now the thing that we Christians have to learn, before shaking our heads over these Jewish leaders, is that there is absolutely no reason to think that sinful men cannot do exactly the same thing *with every subsequent gift from above*—including the very greatest gifts of the Incarnation, the Crucifixion, and the gift of the Spirit at Pentecost. This includes the gifts and sacraments of the new covenant. You say you are baptized in water and the Spirit? That and five bucks, says the prophet, will get you a tall mocha frappuccino.

This may sound disrespectful to some, but it only sounds disrespectful to those who have dragged these things down in order to anchor them to earth, to turn them into something "from below." It only sounds disrespectful to the same kind of person who would have been offended at God's ability to make sons of Abraham out of rocks.

The sacramental history of the church has consisted of large numbers of people making the same mistake that the Jews here had made. Something is given that is wild and heavenly, and we expend all our energies to make it domesticated and earthly. We take the lion of the tribe of Judah—from the upland savannahs of Heaven—and turn it into a tabby cat to keep the bishop's chair warm for him.

And so God raised up heavenly deliverance, a deliverance we call the Reformation. God always raises up such deliverances. We don't ever deserve it, but He always does this. He is the Savior God.

But the same darn thing happened *again*. The five *solas*, heavenly messages of liberation and good news, got turned into a fivefold collection of shibbolethian passwords—or, if you are Reformed Baptist, sibbolethian passwords. And so, over the subsequent centuries, God gave a series of revivals and stirrings that formed the broad outlines of what it means to be a modern evangelical. You must be born again. This was all good, and it too was from heaven. It was not from earth, and so what must earthly men labor to do with this latest heavenly truth? Right—in order to keep the Spirit at bay, they sought to turn "you must be born again" into a subjectivist mantra.

In short, there is absolutely *nothing* that God can give us that we are incapable of turning into an idol. This is precisely why we have to be born again, which is not the same thing as talking about being born again. It turns out that there are a lot of things that we can add to our five bucks in order to get that frappuccino.

If there is a deeper right than being right, and there always is, the question we need to answer is "how deep does it go?" One answer of course is that "the right" goes all the way down, but of more interest to us as sinners is how deep do we have to go before we get to the regenerative right? How far down do we have to go before we can stop? Drill past theology; drill past liturgy; drill past the sacraments; drill past all that stuff. As the song "Denomination Blues" puts it, "You gotta have Jesus, I tell you that's all."

And for those who might want to get huffy about this, thinking that I have somehow disparaged theology, liturgy, sacraments, and all the rest of their mummeries, I would reply with a Pauline "may it never be." You have to drill through those things to know what they even are. Otherwise you are just stuck in a dark tunnel, more's the pity.

GENERATION AND REGENERATION

REGENERATION MEANS BECOMING THE SEED of another—ultimately, starting with one family tree and then acquiring a different one. My father used to be Adam and now he is the second Adam. My father used to be the devil and now he is Abraham. A creature being summoned into being *ex nihilo* is being created. We might say he is being born. We would never say that he was being reborn. Rebirth entails having been in existence already, with another father.

One of the reasons the doctrine of regeneration is so important is because the doctrine of generation is so important. God fashioned man out of the dust of the ground in the first place, but it was the breath of God that established us after His image.

"And the LORD God formed man of the dust of the ground, and breathed into his nostrils the breath of life; and man became a living soul" (Gen. 2:7).

There were two steps here. First God *formed*, and then God *breathed*. When God breathed the breath of life into our first father, it was then that he became a living soul, created in the image of God.

"So God created man in his own image, in the image of God created he him; male and female created he them" (Gen. 1:27).

But this scriptural language of "image" is closely connected to the reality of begetting, or, as we would say it, generation.

"And Adam lived an hundred and thirty years, and *begat* a son *in his own likeness, after his image*; and called his name Seth" (Gen. 5:3).

When Adam had a son, it was a son in his own image, in his own likeness. This is language that plainly echoes what God had done initially with Adam. Adam had a son after his own image just as God had a son after His own image. This means Adam was the son of God by *some species* of generation. Please note an emphasis on *some species*—this is not said in any way that would call into question the unique status of Jesus, the only begotten Son of God. But in *some* sense, Adam was son of God by generation. Luke makes this point:

"Which was the son of Enos, which was the son of Seth, which was the son of Adam, which was the son of God" (Luke 3:38).

The way it was with Adam downstream was also the way it was with Adam one generation upstream. And keep in mind that Adam means *man*, or mankind. We may therefore read it as "mankind, the son of God."

He was a created and begotten son, but he was the kind of son concerning which Arianism would have been just fine—there was a time when Adam was not. Because of this, he was vulnerable to sin. When Adam sinned, *what he was* sinned. He was a son of God who sinned. This meant that a new form of generation was established. In some sense, the sons of God became sons of the devil. The mechanism that accomplished this was the mechanism of separating us, as a race, from the life of God.

"Having the understanding darkened, being *alienated from the life of God* through the ignorance that is in them, because of the blindness of their heart" (Eph. 4:18).

We have lived ever since in the ruins of that original sonship, in the wreckage of our old relationship to the Father.

But because God did not surrender us to the devil entirely, but rather reserved a seed for Himself, this resulted in two lines. There was first *generation*, then *degeneration*, and then, for the elect, *regeneration*. But all who are regenerate are so as a result of a gracious salvage operation conducted on the wreckage of the once glorious human race.

"Of his own will begat he us with the word of truth, that we should be a kind of firstfruits of his creatures" (James 1:18).

The difference between the two lines is stark. Those who are the seed of the woman are characterized by a love of righteousness, and those who are the seed of the serpent are not.

"In this the children of God are manifest, and the children of the devil: whosoever doeth not righteousness is not of God, neither he that loveth not his brother" (1 John 3:9–10; 1 John 2:29; John 8:44).

A denial of the need for a foundational heart change is therefore messing with the narratival arc of the whole story. Because we live in a fallen world, we have a constant tendency to ask the wrong question. In the pro-life debates, for example, we ask "when does human life begin?" which immediately lands us in the ontological categories so beloved by Hellenists everywhere. We should ask a simpler question, as one of our deacons recently did on a survey at a local university campus—"When does fatherhood begin?" This is a potent question *because it does not seek to define human lives apart from their relationships.*

When did we become sons of God? We were generated in His image when He breathed the breath of life into our first father. When did we become objects of wrath, children of the devil? When our first father took the fruit that had been forbidden to him. When were we born again, when were we regenerated? When we believed on the Lord Jesus Christ in truth, moved by the Spirit to do so, and God the Father became our Father once again.

In sum, Jesus says He knows His adversaries are the seed of Abraham in one sense (John 8:37). He and they speak according to the word of their respective fathers (John 8:38). They claim Abraham for a father and, in a sense different from what He has just acknowledged, He denies it (John 8:39). Their works are nothing like Abraham's (John 8:39–40). A few verses later, Jesus states the terrible truth explicitly: They are of their father the devil (John 8:44). This is why He calls them serpents, a brood of vipers. (Matt. 23:33). They are all descended from that ancient serpent. The children of God and the children of the devil are easy to tell apart (1 John 3:10).

Our interest in such passages should not have to do with the wickedness as such, but rather has to do with the divine "paternity suit" that follows on the basis of it. If some covenant members are children of the devil and others are not (as the quotation from 1 John indicates), then there must be a divide of *nature*—these different fathers require different natures, and vice versa. Some may want to reject the very idea of "nature," but such a rejection is problematic in discussions of regeneration because it is impossible in discussions of generation. We generate according to our kinds, we generate according to our *nature*. A fig tree bears figs, according to its nature, and does not bear oranges, which would be contrary to its nature.

FATHER TRANSPLANTS

"BEGAT" IS AN IMPORTANT WORD. In any discussions of regeneration, we have to consistently link regeneration to *generation*, and generation is what happens when people are begotten. The same is true of regeneration. Regeneration means begotten again.

"Of his own will begat he us with the word of truth, that we should be a kind of firstfruits of his creatures" (James 1:18).

"Beloved, let us love one another: for love is of God; and every one that loveth is born of God, and knoweth God" (1 John 4:7).

Regeneration consists of a foundational change in the being of those elected to eternal *life*, and the necessity of this can be seen in the word "begat." But to explain more fully how this is, I have to say something about the nature of the self.

There are two errors to avoid here. One is to assume that each individual as such is self-contained and is provided with a hard shell casing. This gives way too much credit to the self-sufficiency of an autonomous self and is just plain silly. The other error is to think that the self is nothing more than a ganglion of relationships, with no "hard atoms" of individuals between whom such relationships are possible. As a moment of reflection should show, you can't have a chemical reaction without the chemicals. You can't have an electrical current without the poles.

A good illustration of selfhood is provided by a pearl. As a person grows and develops, he does so by means of relationships, and these relationships are critical in constituting who he is. As a boy grows to a man, as he marries, as children are given to him, his selfhood is being built; it is being shaped and constructed. He is now "the brother of . . ." or "the father of . . ." this other person. This is how the pearl grows. But there had to be a grain of sand for this pearl to grow up around. A grain of sand is not a pearl, but there will be no pearl without the grain of sand. So persons are *in* relation, by definition, but persons are not simply those relations *simpliciter*.

But here is where we see the miraculous glory of regeneration. There are many relations that are accretions to the pearl. New friends, a new church body, a new daughter, and so on. But regeneration occurs *when I am given a new Father*. What does that do to my identity? It constitutes as foundational an alteration as can be imagined. It is a new creation.

The hard atom of an individual means there is some sort of continuity, such that a regenerated person could accurately say that *he* used to be of his father the devil, but that now God is *his* Father. There is a common "he" there that spans the conversion. But despite that, a new father still means that there has to be a foundational change in the being of the one who has that new father.

We sometimes say of a converted person that they "met God." This is fine, but we have to be careful not to treat it as though God were just a new friend or acquaintance, a new layer to the pearl. No, *regeneration occurs when someone receives a father transplant.* Can such a thing happen without a total transformation of my identity, of my being? Not a chance.

Imagine two scenarios. One is that I go to a conference and meet a new friend, a man we will call Hank Smith. We become fast friends and remain so for the rest of our lives. What does that do to my identity (and to his)? Well, it is built up further. My friendship with this man is folded into the story of who I am.

But the second scenario is where some weird thing happens such that Hank Smith is suddenly turned into my father, and Jim Wilson is no longer my father. What does that do to my being and identity? Well, it would be totally overhauled, transformed, recreated. *I couldn't be the same person anymore.* Not at all. Regeneration is therefore a total transformation of being and identity. Why? The Spirit of adoption makes us cry out "Abba, *Father!*" We used to be of our father, the devil, and now we have another Father entirely, the Holy One.

In Scripture, there is a basic dividing line between the two races, with different fathers at their respective heads. And incidentally, we must not be confused by the different names that these two lines have down through the course of their history—on the one side we have the devil, or Cain, or Ishmael, seed of the serpent, et al., and on the other we have God, or Abraham, seed of the woman, and so on. But there are just two races—sheep and goats. This division is basic to understanding *history*. It is not just true at the Last Day. We find the seed of the serpent at war with the seed of the woman in the *first* book of the Bible, and not just the last book.

But this dividing line is entirely distinct from (although not unrelated to) the dividing line between the visible church and the world. In other words, it is possible for children of the devil to be deacons and bishops, preachers and laymen, along with being chairs of the women's auxiliary, and depending on what denomination or era of history you are in, being a child of the devil might even be the norm.

And when you put these two truths together—the total transformation of being when someone receives a father transplant, and the fact that numerous members of the visible church have not received such a father transplant—this makes a robust form of evangelicalism a scriptural and logical necessity. Which is, I think, a good reason for embracing it.

So I affirm the importance of relation and would go on to affirm the centrality of a particular relation—our relationship to God. All the questions of regeneration are foundationally questions of relationship—who's your daddy? But I would also argue that a relational ontology understood in this way *requires* the traditional view of regeneration.

Regeneration debates in the New Testament—debates that occur within the visible covenant—should be thought of as a spiritual paternity suit.

> They answered and said unto him, *Abraham is our father.* Jesus saith unto them, If ye were Abraham's children, ye would do the works of Abraham. . . . *Ye do the deeds of your father.* . . . Jesus said unto them, *If God were your Father, ye would love me*: for I proceeded forth and came from God; neither came I of myself, but he sent me. Why do ye not understand my speech? even because ye cannot hear my word. *Ye are of your father the devil,* and the lusts of your father ye will do. (John 8:39, 41, 43–44a)

They were blue star covenant members, these men, and all their sacramental papers were in order. The only problem was that despite everything *they still had the wrong father.* They were therefore, by definition, unregenerate. There are numerous examples of this in the Bible, but here is just one more that should make the point.

> He that committeth sin *is of the devil*; for the devil sinneth from the beginning. For this purpose the Son of God was manifested, that he might destroy the works of the devil. Whosoever is born of God doth not commit sin; *for his seed remaineth* in him: and he cannot sin, *because he is born of God.* In this *the children of God are manifest, and the children of the devil*: whosoever doeth not righteousness is not of God, neither he that loveth not his brother. For this is the message that ye heard from the beginning, that we should love one another. (1 John 3:8–11)

John is not teaching his people to distinguish baptized from unbaptized people. That's too easy. He is assuming a mutual profession of faith here, and he says that time will make the respective paternity issues clear. Yes, we know they are baptized. But who is their father *really*?

So I agree completely with what might be called a (qualified) relational ontology, if by this we mean that who we are is in great part defined by who we're with. But on this question, a central relation is who we are *from*. Some of our relationships, the most important ones, are upstream. Regeneration means that it is possible to have a new upstream. Because we are a race, not created individually, one by one, this means that every professing Christian has to know that it is possible to be catechized, baptized, communed, preached at, made a deacon, and still be a son of the devil.

We were all of us generated. That means that to be saved we must be regenerated. We must have a new Father, and having a new Father is not synonymous with a correct, formal attachment to the Christian church. Everything else follows from that.

So in the Bible, personal identity is not *primarily* a question of some substance inside a man. But each man still has a nature, inherited from his father. So ontology is not a philosophical problem in the Bible, but rather a problem of generation. And when this generation is sinful, the only solution to the problem is regeneration, which is to say, generation by a new Father.

So can we say that God gives exactly the same thing (Himself) to all baptized individuals? And then account for the differences in outcome by saying that God's Spirit works with all individuals differently? I don't think so.

When someone gets married, he gives himself. And he does so, promising that he will *continue* to do so forever. God does the same with His elect. "For I am persuaded, that neither death, nor life, nor angels, nor principalities, nor powers, nor things present, nor things to come, nor height, nor depth, nor any other creature, shall be able to separate us from the love of God, which is in Christ Jesus our Lord" (Rom. 8:38–39).

The elect believe this promise, and it is always fulfilled because the promises are always apprehended by faith. It is not fulfilled for the reprobate covenant member because he does not believe it, and never did. So if God gives Himself to me as my Father, this means that I no longer have the *nature* of my first father, the devil. This is why God continues to be a Father to me. If He gave Himself fully to a reprobate covenant member, then He would give Himself the same way tomorrow, and the day after, and suddenly the reprobate covenant member cannot be considered reprobate.

So long as we acknowledge that there are covenant members who are not saved, then we must necessarily say that God does not give Himself to all in the same way. And this is just another way of saying that some covenant members need to be regenerated.

GOD'S PHONICS PROGRAM

WE HAVE SEEN that questions about spiritual regeneration are tightly tied to questions of spiritual generation. Who is your father? Is it the devil, or is it God the Father? Those are the basic options, and being united to Christ through His church does not mean that the devil might not still be your father.

But those who contend that there is such a thing as a genuine heart transformation—called regeneration, when your paternity changes—have to beware of certain pitfalls. It is not possible for us to read hearts (Luke 8:17), and we ought not to act as though we can. There will be plenty of secrets for the Last Day to reveal. Neither is it possible for us to read the decrees of God (Deut. 29:29), and we should not act as though we can do that either. We can't read hearts, and we can't read the Book of Life.

But from these important truths many have concluded (erroneously) that it is not possible for us to read the *story* we are in. But that is a different thing entirely. Now it is not possible to read a story without reading the characters, and this is something all of us do all the time—although we have been trained for some time now to leave this essential human activity out of the church. But we ought to lean against this, and lean against it hard. We must evaluate the spiritual condition of those around us, and it is essential for pastors to know how to do this properly.

But if you read the story and the characters in it, it will be thought you are trying to read hearts or that you are trying to read the secret counsels of God. But these are different things entirely. Here's how it works:

We all have to make decisions about the character of others, and we do this all the time. We do this based upon their actions, words, placement in the story, timing, facial expressions, tone of voice, and so forth. A man requests the privilege of courting your daughter. Another man asks to be rehired by you after you fired him last summer for constant tardiness. Yet another asks you to vote for him.

Or a preacher asks you to believe . . . what? We are told to do more than reject certain teachings. We are also told to reject the teachers of those teachings, because of their heart condition.

> Beware of false prophets, which come to you in sheep's clothing, but inwardly they are ravening wolves. Ye shall know them by their fruits. Do men gather grapes of thorns, or figs of thistles? Even so every good tree bringeth forth good fruit; but a corrupt tree bringeth forth evil fruit. A good tree cannot bring forth evil fruit, neither can a corrupt tree bring forth good fruit. Every tree that bringeth not forth good fruit is hewn down, and cast into the fire. Wherefore by their fruits ye shall know them. (Matt. 7:15–20)

If you walk away from a false prophet, you are doing so because of your evaluation of the external story—in this case, their fruits. Corrupt fruit means corrupt tree, and good fruit means a good tree. Some false teachers have to be examined closely because they come in sheep's clothing. But your reading of the story tells you that something is "off"—"my, what long ears you have . . ." Now when you have obediently applied this instruction from the Lord, and you no longer tune into Brother Zed's Prosperity Hour, you are doing so on the supposition that he is a wolf. Why? Because Jesus told you to.

When someone does this, he is not "reading hearts." This is not a deductive operation—we do not surmise the nature of the fruit from the nature of the tree. It goes the other way. The fruit is the story, the tree is the inner reality. *Inwardly*, Jesus says, a false prophet is a ravening wolf—but that is not one of your premises. That is the conclusion, and it is the conclusion because it is the moral of the story.

This is not an instance where Jesus can use superpowers to identify false prophets, but we can't, not being Jesus and all. No, this is Jesus telling *us* what to do. He is telling us that—without access to the decrees or the examined prophet's heart laid out before us on a dissecting table—we have the authority to conclude that someone is inwardly a ravening wolf. This is not reading hearts, or reading the decrees. It is reading the story. The outer story reveals the inner man.

Paul does something similar.

"If any man teach otherwise, and consent not to wholesome words, even the words of our Lord Jesus Christ, and to the doctrine which is according to godliness; He is proud, knowing nothing, but doting about questions and strifes of words, whereof cometh envy, strife, railings, evil surmisings, Perverse disputings of men of corrupt minds, and destitute of the truth, supposing that gain is godliness: from such withdraw thyself" (1 Tim. 6:3–5).

This is a conditional—Paul doesn't even know the name of the person who might object to his wholesome words, and yet he knows his motives, which are entirely bad. He expects Timothy (and us) to "withdraw" ourselves from those people, whoever they are, which means that we have *to read the story*.

The biblical pattern of this kind of thing is clear and repeated often. How does Stephen conclude his speech in Acts 7? He concludes with a polemical evaluation of the heart condition of the men who had brought him there. This is not because he had their hearts under a microscope; this is because he knew how this particular story goes. He knew what a protagonist is and what an antagonist is. Here is his peroration, and I call it a bull's eye:

"Ye stiffnecked and uncircumcised in heart and ears, ye do always resist the Holy Ghost: as your fathers did, so do ye" (Acts 7:51).

It is not necessary to claim that Stephen had any special inspiration here (along with an admonition to all of us not to try this sort of thing at home). Inspiration is often a trump card that modernity uses to keep us from being shaped by biblical narrative.

"Beware of dogs, beware of evil workers, beware of the concision. For we are the circumcision, which worship God in the spirit, and rejoice in Christ Jesus, and have no confidence in the flesh" (Phil. 3:2–3).

This is not the apostle saying "there are dogs out there, I know who they are, but I am not telling." This is Paul saying that we should beware of the dogs. But in order to beware of them, you have to be able to identify them. How do you do that? It is not by putting on hyperspiritual glasses that enable you to see the essential dogginess at the core of their heart. You see on the basis of their evil works, their demand for circumcision, and so on. *You read the story.*

Can such judgments ever be wrong? Well, of course they can. That does not mean that we are warned away from making them. The straight line we use to keep ourselves from wronging others in such things is for us to be steeped in the narrative of Scripture. We can test drive our responses with novels and movies. Practice reading stories, because that is what your life is. So the end of the whole endeavor is to live our lives out to the fullest, reading our own story rightly. And there is no way to do this without making conclusions about the internal spiritual condition of others.

Let me illustrate it this way. I was counseling someone recently about how to deal with someone who had been a chronic liar for a long time. How can we tell whether or not to believe them this time? If a chronic liar is insulted that you don't believe him, or don't believe him quickly, then that means that he has not yet repented. But if a chronic liar accepts the disbelief of others with humility and grace, then this means he has repented.

Suppose you have a backslidden Christian, but someone who is truly regenerate. He has backslidden badly, and is utterly miserable, but still in that frame of mind where he is trying to shout down his regenerate misery in a flurry of cocaine and floozies. Cocaine is in there because "flurry of floozies" would be way too much, even for a writer like me. And yet, despite the chaos of sin around him (for some reason) he *knows* that he knows God, and that God is going to get him back any minute now. Has this kind of thing ever happened? You bet it has. Now suppose this man, in this condition, is confronted by a Christian who knew him fifteen years before, back when he was walking with God. Suppose the old friend rebukes him on the basis of the cocaine and floozies, and says something like, "You are not a Christian, and you never were."

The man in sin could know that this was false, and precisely *because* it was false, he would acknowledge that such an assessment was utterly *just*. If the accusation were true (and the man were unregenerate) he would likely be as indignant as a wet cat. "What do you mean, not a Christian? I prayed the prayer at my grandma's knee, and signed the family Bible!" But if he really were a believer, he would know exactly why his confronter was reading the story the way he was reading it.

There is safety in the way we are taught to read. It is part of God's phonics program.

THE HOLY SPIRIT'S COMMONPLACE BOOK

LET'S BEGIN WITH A SHORT CHAIN OF VERSES, with the emphases all mine, followed by just a couple of observations.

> But if I with *the finger of God* cast out devils, no doubt the kingdom of God is come upon you. (Luke 11:20)

> But if I cast out devils *by the Spirit of God*, then the kingdom of God is come unto you. (Matt. 12:28)

> And he gave unto Moses, when he had made an end of communing with him upon mount Sinai, two tables of testimony, tables of stone, *written with the finger of God*. (Ex. 31:18; cf. Deut. 9:10)

> Who also hath made us able ministers of the new testament; not of the letter, but of the spirit: for the letter killeth, but *the spirit giveth life*. But if the ministration of death, written and engraven in stones, was glorious, so that the children of Israel could not stedfastly behold the face of Moses for the glory of his countenance; which glory was to be done away: How shall not the ministration of the spirit be rather glorious? (2 Cor. 3:6–8)

> But this shall be the covenant that I will make with the house of Israel; After those days, saith the LORD, *I will put* my law in their inward parts, *and write it* in their hearts; and will be their God, and they shall be my people. (Jer. 31:33)

> For this is the covenant that I will make with the house of Israel after those days, saith the Lord; *I will put* my laws into their

mind, *and write them* in their hearts: and I will be to them a God, and they shall be to me a people. (Heb. 8:10; 10:16)

Forasmuch as ye are manifestly declared to be the epistle of Christ ministered by us, written not with ink, *but with the Spirit* of the living God; not in tables of stone, but in fleshy tables of the heart. (2 Cor. 3:3)

And I will give them one heart, and I will put a new spirit within you; and I will take the stony heart out of their flesh, and will give them an heart of flesh. (Ezek. 11:19)

This is an *a fortiori* argument, a "how much more" argument. If God can quicken and glorify stone by writing on it with His own finger, then how much more will human hearts be glorified, quickened, made alive, and regenerated when the finger of God, the Holy Spirit Himself, writes on them? What is it to be born again? It is to become the Holy Spirit's commonplace book.

When He does this, He is transforming us into a renewed, true humanity. When Jesus is teaching Nicodemus about the absolute necessity of the new birth, Nicodemus does not understand what He is talking about. In response to that bafflement, Jesus says this:

"If I have told you earthly things, and ye believe not, how shall ye believe, if I tell you of heavenly things" (John 3:12)?

Catch that? Being born again is *not* about "heavenly things." It is not the creation of heavenly ambrosia for us to sip during the remaining days of our earthly toil. It is the creation of earthly wine from earthly water. Heaven *acts* when a man is born again, but heaven is not transferred. It was supernatural power that Jesus exercised when He turned water to wine, but the result was not supernatural wine. It was regular wine.

Jesus indicates to Nicodemus that there are heavenly doctrines that would stagger him, but we can't go there until the earthly ABCs are mastered first. He was having trouble in the earthly kindergarten, and so we have to postpone the heavenly graduate school.

So regeneration is not an esoteric doctrine. It is not something we are allowed to postpone discussion of until later. It is the *sine qua non* of being able to discuss *anything* later. If a man is not born again, he will not be able to see the kingdom, much less sit down in that kingdom to learn the things that Jesus said were so far beyond us now.

This is because when we are born again, a dramatic miracle happens. When we are born again, *we are being turned into people*.

The Holy Spirit is sovereign in His work. The Wind blows where He wishes and is not bottled up by anything whatever that *we* can do—whether we are talking about decision cards or baptismal fonts. Understanding this is a function of basic piety, and we have countless passages in Scripture that reinforce this reality by talking about things like sacrifices, sacraments, music, miracles, temples, and so on, with a sublime kind of disrespect. God can make sons of Abraham out of your driveway gravel, which is not a good reason to decorate your sanctuary with the magic driveway gravel.

But we need to take a moment to address a theological and anthropological aspect to it. If you believe that the Spirit can depart from a man who is "as converted as the next guy," there are only two basic directions you can go. Either this was the determination of the individual, being able to say to the Spirit, in effect, "You must go," or it was the determination of the Spirit saying, "I will go now." The former is Arminianism, and the latter reduces, at the end of its theological pilgrimage, to a form of fatalism.

The key is found in the phrase "as the next guy." In the former set up, he is as "born again" as the next guy, but he loses it. Regeneration is reversible. In the latter, he is as set apart by baptism as the next guy. Regeneration is understood differently than the evangelical Arminian understands it, but there is agreement on one thing—whatever it is, it is reversible. This is Augustinian, not Wesleyan, but after we have rendered all due respect to that great Christian, vastly my superior, we still have to differ with it. In this view, election cannot be reversed, but regeneration can be.

The question is this—in either framework is there a group of people to whom God keeps all His promises *regardless*, and can those people know who they are?

I want to argue that wisdom is vindicated by her children and that the promises of God are given to those in whom the promises of God are realized. When Jesus went through the land healing all manner of diseases, how could we tell which ones were healed? Well . . . I would argue . . . the ones who actually got better.

Every blind man that Jesus touched could *see* after that. But not every blind man touched by the waters of baptism can see after that. Some of them remain as blind as all get out. Now if every third blind man that Jesus touched physically remained blind, the two who could see would still be a remarkable testimony of His power. His miraculous power would still testify to who He was. But, at the end of the day, we would nevertheless have to give an account of those who were "healed" without being actually healed. Right? We would need a theological category for that.

That is the situation we have with those set apart to Christ by baptism. Some of them can see the glories of His grace, and some of them are still bumping into things. Some of those who bump into things have gotten so good at it that they have set up their Blind Guide Tour Guide Service (BGTGS) and, as in the first century, business is brisk (Matt. 15:14). This means that there are covenant members who surrounded themselves with all the apparatus of the covenant but who failed to com-bine what they had *with faith* (Heb. 4:2). We therefore have the category we need—that of unregenerate covenant member.

Now someone is going to say that this reduces my faith in God to a faith in something that occurred in me, something *inside* me, and that this detracts from the objectivity of the death of Jesus for sinners. Are we not supposed to look away, to Jesus? Well, sure. But when we look away to Jesus, one of the things that happens is that *we see.*

"He answered and said, Whether he be a sinner or no, I know not: one thing I know, that, whereas I was blind, now I see" (John 9:25).

When he testified that he could now see, in what way could that possibly detract from the glory of the one who *healed* him?

There is a pitfall that some have fallen into, the mistake of trying to have faith in their own faith. Sure, and so let's not do that. Blind men healed should look at Jesus, and then at the world. They should spend very little time trying to look at their own eyeballs. You look *with* your eyeballs, not *at* them. But let us not, for fear of this mistake, make another opposing mistake, equally ludicrous—the mistake of pretending that blind men get to testify to His healing grace and power.

EVERY ATOM SUPERGLUED IN PLACE

ONE VERY PERTINENT QUESTION TO ASK about this emphasis on regeneration as a change of nature is whether it represents an attempt to find a fixed point within the created order, which would make it a species of idolatry. The reason this is a great question is that the human mind, as Calvin noted, is an idol factory, and can make an idol out of *anything*. It is possible to take the law "no idolatry," absolutize it, and turn *that* into an idol. But enough about Islam.

There can only be one fixed point in the created world, and that is the Word of God. The grass withers, the flower fades, but the Word of the Lord endures forever (1 Pet. 1:24). But note what this does—the constant (considered as absolute) is the Word of God. But this Word fastens *something* in the created order. It is a secure truth, nailed down by God's Word, that grass withers. That is the way it is—not because ultimate and autonomous witherdom resides within the grass, but rather because God spoke it that way.

We don't usually fall into the idolatry mistake with things that wither, though. Here is the temptation from a more obvious and tempting direction. God "by his strength *setteth fast the mountains*; being girded with power"(Ps. 65:6). When God makes the mountains fast, it becomes possible for men to establish the high places, and forget the God who alone created the high places. Here is a fixed point in the created order, but it is only fixed because of the Word of God. Forget that, and you're sunk.

Scripture cannot be broken (John 10:35), and this is why the bones of Christ could not be broken (John 19:36)—it was not because the bones of Christ were a fixed point in the created order, made out of celestial titanium.

"Let all the earth fear the Lord: Let all the inhabitants of the world stand in awe of him. For he spake, and it was done; *He commanded, and it stood fast*" (Ps. 33:8–9).

But as soon as something is standing fast (because of the Word of God, and only because of the Word of God), the sinful heart of man can come along and make an idol out of it. "Look how sturdy that is!" But the fact that it is so sturdy— defined, placed, fixed, and fastened by *God*—does not make it God. But this *also* means that we, not being God ourselves, cannot point to the mutability of all things ("the grass withers, does it not?") and turn that into an argument for sex-change operations. "*Everything* changes, man!"

The reason we cannot do this is because the Word of God has defined the image of God in mankind as "male and female" (Gen. 1:27). He *fixed* it that way. The pomosexuals want the created order to be infinitely malleable, while the idolatrous tra- ditionalists want "traditional marriage" precisely because they want a fixed point within the created order, without reference to God. And that move is impotent at best, deadly at worst, and sinful all the time. Every attempt to find a fixed point within the created order apart from the triune God is idolatry. But it is also idolatry to try to pretend that He hasn't spoken His certainties into our world. We don't like His certainties. Uncertainties make a nice little fog to sin in. Idolizing the fog is no better.

So are there fixed points in the created world? Yes, when God speaks them. When He creates all the species according to their kinds, that's the way it is. When He put the Rocky

Mountains there, that's where they stayed. But the world is only stable *because there is no foundation for stability within it*. But once you introduce the Words of God, how gloriously stable it becomes! Every hair is numbered, every sparrow noted, and every atom superglued in place.

Let's bring this back to the matter of regeneration. Regeneration is God speaking. It is a matter of God creating. The new birth is a new creation (2 Cor. 5:17; Gal. 6:15).

"For God, who commanded the light to shine out of darkness, hath shined in our hearts, to give the light of the knowledge of the glory of God in the face of Jesus Christ" (2 Cor. 4:6).

This is like one of those mountains that God commanded to stand fast. And evangelicals who make regeneration into a high place, where they worship their own feelings and subjective experiences, have indeed fallen into idolatry. They have gone and left out the whole point. But those who look to Christ, and who know that nothing in this sorry joint of a fallen world can stay put unless *He* is telling it to, are not guilty of idolatry. Just the reverse.

Why? The just shall live by faith, and that means faith in what He *said*.

So when I say that regeneration entails a foundational change in our nature, what do I mean? What *is* our nature? What we need to remember going into it is that we are not trying to veer off from biblical categories into philosophical ones, but rather wanting to preserve our right to speak as the Bible does, using the illustrations and metaphors that the Bible uses.

The images of Scripture encourage us to think in terms of the final cash out, the bottom line. There are two and only two destinations for human beings—Heaven and Hell—and everything else pales when that final destiny is taken into account. We do not speak the words that will be spoken at the end of history in the middle of history (how could we?), but we should speak our words now in *light* of the fact that such words will in fact be spoken. We do not foolishly pronounce the judgment itself simply by remembering in faith that there will *be* such a judgment.

> And before him shall be gathered all nations: and he shall separate them one from another, *as a shepherd divideth his sheep from the goats*: And he shall set the sheep on his right hand, but the goats on the left. (Matt. 25:32–33)

> Not every one that saith unto me, Lord, Lord, shall enter into the kingdom of heaven; but he that doeth the will of my Father which is in heaven. Many will say to me in that day, Lord, Lord, have we not prophesied in thy name? and in thy name have cast out devils? and in thy name done many wonderful works? And then will I profess unto them, *I never knew you*: depart from me, ye that work iniquity. (Matt. 7:21–23)

This judgment, when it falls, will be *binary*. There will be sheep and there will be goats. There will be the "good and faithful servants" and there will be the "I never knew you" group, and there will be no remainder.

Moreover, the Bible teaches that all of us are by nature objects of wrath (Eph. 2:3), which means that *all* of us are goats to begin with. In order to get any sheep at all, there has to be a miracle of some sort, changing some from the nature of a goat to the nature of a sheep. You can't get a sheep out of a goat otherwise. This is what I am referring to when I speak of a change in nature.

I have occasionally used the word *ontological* in describing this kind of change of our nature, and this might mislead some. But by ontological I do not mean that some kind of ontos chip is embedded deep in our souls, and in regeneration God swaps it out. *Ontos* is simply the Greek participle for being, and *being* a goat is different than *being* a sheep.

These illustrations all come from *within nature*. A sheep is a natural animal, as is a goat. When a man is regenerated, he is not transformed into some kind of angelic demigod from another realm. No, he is changed into a *man*, and the material out of which God performed this miracle was the remains of a man, the ruins of a man. This is not a change from nature into grace; it is a change from broken nature to restored nature, and the change is accomplished *by grace*. We are not changed *into* grace, we are transformed *by* grace.

When Jesus changed the water into wine, it was natural water and the result was natural wine. The miracle was in the verb, not in the resultant noun. Jesus didn't turn water into ambrosia. So it is important to note that I am not at all urging any attempted escape from nature—I am saying that God's grace is necessary to get us fully back into nature. There *is* an attempted escape from nature going on, and the tunnel is sin, which will at some point empty out into the outer darkness.

I recall many years ago picking up a Christian book which had a schematic diagram of a human being's innards—soul, will, body, etc, all within an easily understood circle. My thought at the time was to wonder how anyone could presume to be that specific about how we are put together. The spirit of man is *mysterious*. "The spirit of man is the candle of the Lord, searching all the inward parts of the belly" (Prov. 20:27). We can learn a great deal about ourselves, but not in trite and superficial ways.

And so I am not attempting anything so tidy here. The nature of a man does go down to mysterious depths, *but it also extends out to the border of his skin*. His nature includes the fact that he is male, that he is Asian, that he has black hair, and so on. It also includes his visible actions, actions which reveal the nature of his heart. A bunch of it is mysterious, but a lot of it isn't.

Our generation places a lot more faith in genetic determinism than they ought to, and so we ought to lean heavily against the idea that a human being's genetic code is the suitcase of his nature, and all that happens in the course of his life is the unpacking of that suitcase. I reject that idea with shouts of loud scorn. But this means that I am not saying that when a man is regenerated, what is happening is that God is magically altering the contents of the suitcase, and that's all. Our beings, our selves, our lives, contain a "hard atom" of what and who we are to begin with, but the rest of our story is shaped and defined by our relationship to others, particularly in relationship to God.

When we begin our (goatish) journey, the devil is our father. We start off in that relation, which cannot end well. When we are converted, when we are turned around, God becomes our Father. In order for that relationship to be established, we must be born again. Otherwise, the devil is still our father.

So, then, to conclude, when we are changed, the Bible encourages us (requires us) to use language that in any other circumstance would be describing a change of *nature* (we are former goats, vipers, pigs, dogs, etc.) Our nature is changed, and the way it happens is mysterious. But one thing is certain—the change is not limited to something outside us. The changes do not skim along the surface.

It is entirely a supernatural work, as Dort puts it. It is "most powerful and most pleasing, a marvelous, hidden, and inexpressible work, which is not lesser than or inferior in power to that of creation or of raising the dead." It is not a natural work in the sense of continuing our old natures. Neither is it a supernatural work in the sense that it takes and removes us from the created order. We are still men and women. But, as Bavinck says, it "penetrates their inmost being and re-creates them, in principle, according to the image of God. It is therefore in a class of its own, simultaneously ethical and natural (supernatural), powerful and most pleasing." And amen to that.

UGLY DIES

GEORGE MACDONALD ONCE FAMOUSLY SAID that obedience is the great opener of eyes. But obedience has to come from an obedient heart, and in order to have obedient hearts, we must have new hearts. This brings us (yet again) to the foundational necessity of the new birth. Without that reality, there is absolutely nothing we can do to make the Christian life work. Whatever we try to make it work, without the new birth, we are like monkeys pushing buttons on a broken cash register. Nothing happens. There is only one thing to do, apart from repentance, which is to *pretend* that something really is happening, which is an easy reach for monkey brains with monkey hearts.

Those buttons might be ethical—giving up everything for the poor, but without love, which is a big Pauline goose egg (1 Cor. 13:3). Those buttons might be the fancy dress parade of sacramentalism, and yet the Lord wonders aloud who asked us to come around to trample noisily in His courts (Isa. 1:12). Those buttons might be doctrinal, as we think we have figured out how to plump up *all* the cushions on Moses' seat, and we are quite cozy there as we issue directives for others (Matt. 23:2).

But the natural man, the unconverted man, the unregenerate man, is the same kind of man whether he is inside the covenant or outside it, with the difference that reprobates inside the covenant have greater condemnation. They are sinning against greater light, and to whom much is given, much is required. But they do not have a heart that can meet the greater requirement, and they cannot manufacture the heart they need. If we could repent and believe with our old hearts, then why do we need new ones?

When a natural man is converted, all of a sudden everything that was an opaque mystery to him before becomes a delight, with light shed all over it. The Bible turns into English, the worship of God in a way that honors Him becomes a delight, and the poor turn into Jesus Christ, instead of a rung in somebody's heaven ladder. Before conversion, these things are covered in darkness. He cannot understand them for they are spiritually discerned.

"But the natural man receiveth not the things of the Spirit of God: for they are foolishness unto him: neither can he know them, because they are spiritually discerned" (1 Cor. 2:14).

And anybody who believes that such a "natural man" can only exist outside the confines of the visible church is an observer who doesn't get out much. Churches are shot through with such unconverted parishioners—and by this I mean to indicate Roman Catholic churches, Eastern Orthodox churches, Lutheran churches, Reformed churches, and evangelical churches. Whatever are we to do with this? Well, we should start by preaching the gospel to everybody. And by "preach the gospel," incidentally, I do not mean the common travesty of rounding up the truly converted and preaching in such a way as to unsettle *their* confidence. Once upon a time, as I have heard tell, gospel was thought to mean good news.

Once converted, everything that used to be "law" is now gift, it is now grace. This includes the grace of dying. The privilege of participating in the cross of Jesus is a privilege, it is a gift. Mortification is grace, it is gift, it is goodness. *Mortification is a great kindness.*

There are three levels of "dying," all of which are grace, which I will illustrate using the metaphor of a garden. The first happens when the Lord rototills a weed patch and turns it into a dirt patch for a garden. This is the foundational mortification, the death of the old man (which was the weed patch) and the creation of a new man (which is a garden). This is what happens at true conversion (Rom. 6:3).

The second kind of death occurs within the Christian life and can be described as the digging up of big weeds in the garden. Paul, speaking to *Christians*, tells them that they have already died (level one) and that their life is now hid with Christ in God (Col. 3:3). But then a few verses later, he tells them to mortify the really big weeds (Col. 3:5). This means that real Christians can struggle with big sins. What problems do these saints have, which Paul calls here their "members which are on the earth?" They include "fornication, uncleanness, inordinate affection, evil concupiscence, and covetousness, which is idolatry." All pretty bad. But God's grace is with us still, and if we are converted, we will love the idea of having these big weeds pulled. If we are not truly converted, we will hate the idea. Hatred of this second level of mortification means that we actually hated the first level, which means that we have not really received the first level. Anybody who loves the weeds is still a weed patch—regardless of their attachment to the visible church. Loving your sin while loving Jesus is an exercise that the Bible calls kidding yourself.

And the third level of mortification is a godly Christian going out to the garden at 6 a.m. to weed every day. There has never been a gardener in the history of the world who went out into his garden at dawn to find weeds who couldn't find any. What diligent gardener ever walked over his garden without finding a single weed? He always finds *something*, but the weeds (however toxic in their nature) are the size of his thumbnail. They are pulled a lot more easily than the knee-high weeds were. This is an ongoing process of mortification (Rom. 8:13), and it too is a grace.

Bonhoeffer said that when Christ calls a man, he bids him come and die. A gracious heart hears this message and leaps for joy. An ungracious heart hears it, and looks for a place to hide. *Anything* but death. Scripture teaches us, and history shows us, that the very best hiding places, at least for a brief time, are found in the things of God—the church, the Bible, the sacraments, the catechism, the ministry, the Internet theology debates, the church splits over a bunch of nothing, the mercy ministries, and of course, the venerable tradition of the fathers. Those fathers, incidentally, can be found both in the Jerusalem chamber at Westminster *and* in the Syrian desert.

So here is the good news. So hear the gospel—ugly dies, and loveliness rises.

SPEAKING BIBLICALLY

IT MAY WELL BE THAT SOME OBJECT to my method of pitting certain biblical themes against one another—as though I can retain a traditional evangelical suspicion of form and ritual while seeking to promote a return for liturgical form and ritual. And at first glance, it certain looks as though there *might* be a problem with it.

Now (because of my fondness for the law of noncontradiction) I agree that we cannot become formal and retain our hostility to form in the same way and in the same respect. I don't want to try to affirm L and not L. But can we not become formal in the ways that the Bible requires and retain our hostility to form in the ways that the Bible requires? God mandates the construction of the Temple; God levels the Temple. God requires sacrifice; God requires mercy and *not* sacrifice. God requires us to rend our garments; God requires us to rend our hearts, *not* our garments. And so on.

The Bible *routinely* opposes things that are not *necessarily* opposed to each other. Pastoral opposition is not the same thing as logical opposition. This is why we must retain our right to speak biblically, even if it creates tensions in our systematic theology—or in our liturgics.

I want to cheerfully concur that when liturgy is enacted out of real love for Jesus, God doesn't have any problems with it. In other words, I grant the very reasonable point that the "liturgical" churches aren't (in this sense) liturgical enough. But liturgy (I want to argue) is a form of wealth, and those who are rich in this present world need to be regularly warned not to set their hopes on riches, which are so easily destroyed. So the fat cats who abuse wealth are really doing so, but their problem (following the structure of this argument, with which I agree) is that they are not rich *enough*—they are not rich toward God. But they are rich enough to be dazzled by something they oughtn't have been dazzled by. And the formal churches that are spiritually anemic are liturgical enough to be distracted by the form of religion, without the power.

But isn't there a way to look "through" that doesn't treat the means as therefore dispensable? Jesus chided the Jews because they searched the Scriptures, and yet the Scriptures bore witness to Christ. They stared at the Bible as though it were a mural, when it is actually a window. But to say this is quite a separate thing from saying that windows are unnecessary.

Nobody gets Jesus "raw." He is in, with, under, on the other side of, and on this side of, everyone who has real faith. Amen. It is always both/and. But when unbelieving hearts separate them and want the form of religion without heart transformation, God's judgment on such people is *always* to attack their props—because that's all they have. And since He attacks such props (when they are props, as often happens), then His ministers have to do the same.

There are no raw sacraments and no raw Scriptures either. Jesus must be present, but because of unbelief it is often the case that He isn't. Faith is what keeps it all together. So this concern of mine is not faith attacking faith; it is faith attacking the subtleties of unbelief.

If we speak with biblical balance, then God will keep real confidence in His ordinances from being undermined. Just as biblical warnings about apostasy don't undermine a proper confidence in the perseverance of the saints, so also if a minister of the sacraments isn't afraid to put his foot through the side of a false notion of the sacraments, the right kind of faith in the congregation will be strengthened, not diluted.

The problem is never "this or that" niggle with the liturgy. The problem is that God cannot endure iniquity and solemn assembly, and the more correct the solemn assembly is, the worse it is. That is what the prophets attacked, and also what I am attacking—covenant renewal worship and porn slavery, covenant renewal and wife abuse, covenant renewal and hookers, etc.

When the men of Israel weep and wail because God is not hearing their prayers, not receiving their sacrifices, the identified problem was not their liturgy—the problem was their *lives*. So if there is a biblically defensible liturgy coupled with biblically indefensible lives, this is a routine maneuver by sinful men to try to put God into their debt by doing just what He told them to, as though it were a paint-by-numbers kit. And since that is how the sinful heart of man loves to think, in Scripture God takes their paint-by-numbers kit out of their hands, and pitches it away from Him in holy disgust. They are bewildered because He was the one who ordained it in the first place. And so Jesus said to them, "Go and find out what this means . . ."

And this is why we must return to the necessity of speaking to the assembled people of God in just the way the Bible does.

On the one hand . . .

"Or do you not know that the unrighteous will not inherit the kingdom of God? Do not be deceived: neither the sexually immoral, nor idolaters, nor adulterers, nor men who practice homosexuality, nor thieves, nor the greedy, nor drunkards, nor revilers, nor swindlers will inherit the kingdom of God" (1 Cor. 6:9–10).

And then on the other . . .

"And such were some of you. But you were washed, you were sanctified, you were justified in the name of the Lord Jesus Christ and by the Spirit of our God" (1 Cor. 6:11).

We have to grasp both poles of this tension, and the Spirit makes it harmonious. We have to say to the people, as I do every week at the Table, "Come, and welcome, to Jesus Christ." And we also have to tell them that there is a *pro forma* way of coming to the sacrament that just accelerates the hell-bound.

As I write that last sentence, I am most eager not to have it taken as encouragement to morbid introspection by the uberpious. I am talking about the guys getting lap dances, the angry husbands, the men with silk undies getting hormone shots, and so on. Paul says that the works of the flesh (which result in not inheriting the kingdom) are *manifest*. So this is not about reading hearts at all.

The New Testament writers, who were dealing with a fledgling church that was not long gone in apostasy, showed us how to keep things real through their warnings. We find *chapters* of warnings.

IN SUMMARY

So here are the three basic points I have been seeking to make, helpfully arranged in a comparatively small but surprisingly spacious carrying case.

1. The need to speak biblically to the people of God is central. But this must be done *tota et sola Scriptura*, and not just *sola Scriptura*. Not just scriptural expressions only, but *all* scriptural expressions, and in this case, all scriptural expressions that are addressed to the people of God, in their various and varying conditions. This means that there is a sense in which we must insist that the people of God can be divided into two groups—tares and wheat (Matt. 13:25ff), sheep and goats (Matt. 25:32), those who have the Spirit and those who do not (1 John 4:13), and so on. Examples can be multiplied and throughout this book have been.

   And, at the same time, there is another sense (a different sense) in which we must insist that genuine branches can be cut out of the Vine which is Christ (John 15:1–6) or lopped off the olive tree of the new Israel (Rom. 11:17ff), or that wheat can fail to grow to fruition (Matt. 13:3ff). In these cases, there is a sense in which they share *branchness* or *wheatness* with the elect. So some biblical metaphors point to the nature of the thing (tares or wheat) while others point to the outcome of the thing (fruitless branches or fruitful branches). We must not pit these metaphors against one another for the sake of a system; we must use them all in different circumstances, as appropriate. We do not juxtapose them and choose which set we want to preach on. We layer them, accepting them all.

2. We must remember one particular foundational point of continuity between old and new covenants. Sons of Belial are covenant members who ought to know the Lord, but who through their sin and rebellion refuse to know the Lord (1 Sam. 2:12). But the perennial temptation for us in the new covenant is to draw *contrasts* with the Israelites at just the places where the New Testament requires us to draw parallels (1 Cor. 10:1–11; Heb. 3:1–4:13; Rom. 11:17ff). "Watch out for *this*," the apostolic writers repeatedly tell us. "This really tripped up the Jews, and you guys could *easily* fall into the same thing."

    Now clearly there is a glorious discontinuity in the fulfillment of all things in Christ. But at the same time, we must not emphasize that discontinuity *in any way that allows us to dispense with the warnings* that the New Testament repeatedly gives us. Those warnings highlight the fact that not all Israel are Israel, which means that—if we are following—not all Christians are Christians.

3. The issues surrounding regeneration should not be settled by looking at the biblical uses of the word regeneration only. It needs to be settled by looking at the thought group of generation/regeneration. Who is your father? Regeneration is not a spiritual joy juice; regeneration is what replaces your previous *generation*, from Adam to the new Adam, from the devil to Abraham, from Cain to

Abel, from Hagar to Sarah, and so forth. This is why it is possible for Jesus to acknowledge that the Pharisees were sons of Abraham in one sense (John 8:37) and sons of the devil in quite another (John 8:44). Life is simple. If God were their Father (as they claimed), they would have loved Jesus (John 8:42). Once we come to grips with the fact that covenant members can hate Jesus, and that many of them do, a robust evangelicalism becomes a scriptural necessity.

We must be in a position to say to a baptized covenant member who is in high rebellion against every article in the Apostles' Creed and in settled noncompliance with every one of the Ten Commandments that there is a sense in which he is a Christian (John 8:37), and there is quite another sense in which, if he is a Christian, then I am the erstwhile queen of Norway (John 8:44).

PART FOUR

DOCTRINAL LEFTOVERS

AN EVANGELICAL ODDITY

As a friend and I discussed regeneration, he wondered at my use of *evangelical* to describe my position, when many Calvinistic evangelicals (think Lloyd-Jones here) would certainly balk at some of my applications of it.

First, I identify as an evangelical because of what I consider to be shared foundational assumptions about *what regeneration is*. Try this: "Regeneration is a sovereign act of the Holy Spirit which monergistically transforms a child of the devil into a child of God, and which necessarily results in a life of repentance and faith being subsequently manifest in that individual." How's that? Can I get an amen?

Now most of our problems come from attempts to get the repentance and faith into an antecedent position to the transformation by the Spirit. But it is regeneration → repentance → faith, not repentance → faith → regeneration. I have to hear the gospel preached before I can believe it, but I don't have to hear the gospel preached before the Spirit *disposes my heart* to listen to that preacher. At some point prior to Mary speaking, the Spirit disposed the heart of John the Baptist in the womb to leap when he heard the words of Mary's salutation (Luke 1:44). Regeneration is prior; regeneration comes first.

Like all good monergistic Calvinists I believe that we repent and believe because we were already reborn, and we are not reborn because we did something first. If we have to do something first, this is bad news for those of us who can't "do" anything.

That being the case, if that is an acceptable evangelical definition of regeneration, then why can it not be applied to little ones? If it is a monergistic gift, bearing fruit as age-appropriate, what restricts God from giving that gift early on?

Now I know that my baptist friends and my Banner of Truth friends would differ with such applications as I am going to make here—but I can make them without changing a word in our shared definition of regeneration. This means that I am pushing this definition into the corners, but applying it more extensively is not an alteration. We have been together for a while, playing our guitars on the porch, and, true, I have headed for Nashville in search of a record deal, but I am *still playing the same song.*

What is that song? Human beings are all descended from their father Adam and are objects of wrath by nature—every last one of them. In order for that condition to change, God must unilaterally do it, and when He does this, the life of the convert exhibits what He has done. If a person goes to Heaven when he dies, this means, necessarily, that God intervened at some point in his life—the time stamp of which is *usually unknown to us,* but which is *always* known to the God who did the intervening.

For us to say that the sovereign God can't really start this work of His until after the kid has memorized the Heidelberg Catechism is to do two things: It is to make a kid memorize the Heidelberg, and it is to demonstrate for him how to effectively disregard what it teaches. God is *God*! We do not get to cordon off our covenant children with those yellow caution tapes, so that the God of all covenant mercies won't jump the gun. "There He goes again . . . forgiving people *early.*"

Allowing that God starts early, and does so lots of times, is not *culturally* evangelical. Most evangelicals don't think this way, I cheerfully admit, but when they become *more* evangelical, they will. It is not culturally evangelical, but it is doctrinally evangelical. My evangelicalism is Lloyd-Jonesian, and with its hair in a braid. It is not culturally that way, which is fine, and I don't have his swell accent either. And I can't preach like he could. But in what I am saying we have agreement in two essential things—God is God, and the new birth is an absolute necessity for every last person.

What aspect of our shared definition would I not be applying? I believe I am applying it consistently, and across the board. To affirm the reality of regenerate zygotes (which I do affirm, lots of them) is not a contradiction of evangelicalism simply because the zygote doesn't have legs yet and cannot walk the aisle at the invitation. The aisle, the invitation, the playing of "Just As I Am," the waiting for a certain birthday, all that stuff, are not essential to evangelicalism. They are merely cultural trappings, some innocent, some not so much. The monergistic work of the Holy Spirit *is* essential to a true and robust evangelicalism, and the Bible tells us that He often starts in on that work pretty darn early.

> But thou art he that took me out of the womb: *Thou didst make me hope when I was upon my mother's breasts.* I was cast upon thee from the womb: *Thou art my God from my mother's belly.* (Ps. 22:9–10)

> *Out of the mouth of babes and sucklings hast thou ordained strength* because of thine enemies, that thou mightest still the enemy and the avenger. (Ps. 8:2)

> When I call to remembrance *the unfeigned faith that is in thee,* which dwelt first in thy grandmother Lois, and thy mother Eunice; and I am persuaded that in thee also ... And that from *a child* [*brephos*, fetus, infant] thou hast known the holy scriptures, which are able to make thee wise unto salvation through faith which is in Christ Jesus. (2 Tim. 1:5; 3:15)

Now what about those people who agree with this on paper, but who never experience it? Wisdom is vindicated by her

children. If a kid was baptized, educated in the covenant, catechized until his eyes bulged out, and all the rest of that drill,
and apostatized in a terrible flame-out as soon as he left home,
what does that do to the promises? *Nothing!* Let God be true,
and every man a liar. But notice what saying this necessitates.
It requires us to acknowledge that when the words don't come
true, it was the men who were lying, not God. It also requires
us to acknowledge that *somebody* was lying. Nobody goes to
Hell on a misunderstanding.

Faithfulness is as faithfulness does. If I were a televangelist
healing folks on the teevee, and everybody were leaving the
stage in the same wheelchair that brought them there, at some
point I ought to reexamine my textual premises.

It is the same kind of thing here. The works of the flesh
are manifest, which in the Greek means that dirty deeds are
apparent. When that kind of heart is made manifest, we can
see that God is not breaking His Word, but rather that He is
keeping it. Those who live this way will not inherit the kingdom of God, and we shouldn't care if they were baptized by
John the Baptist three times in the morning, and then spent
the afternoon playing with the ax he left at the root of the tree.

REGENERATION DEFINED ONCE MORE

So we earlier defined *regeneration* as being given the efficacious gift of a new father. Since like begets like, having a new father means having a new heart, which is a shorthand way of describing the new birth. But having defined it that way, I know that I shall be asked for definitions of *new* and *heart*. So I will come back to that, at least in principle.

Baptism is the sign and seal of that which it represents, and one of the things it represents (and thereby signs, seals, exhibits, and confers) is regeneration. It does this for all worthy receivers, who are identified as such by their evangelical faith. That faith may not appear for many years after an infant is baptized, which is just fine by the Westminster divines, who maintain that the efficacy of baptism is not at all duct-taped to the time of its administration.

Now if the baptized infant never comes to faith, then his covenantal union with Christ, sealed in his baptism, is the basis of a more severe judgment against him, for to whom much is given much is required. Baptism is never empty; baptism is never a meaningless act. I deny that baptism operates *ex opere operato* for blessing, but I do affirm that it operates *ex opere operato* in formally ratifying the baptizand's relationship to the covenant.

Such an unconverted person has Abraham as a covenantal father, as his baptism plainly testifies, but his lying heart shows that the devil is his *actual* father. This individual's sin has separated what God intended to be together—covenant responsibilities and covenant faithfulness. But covenant faithlessness in no way removes or erases covenant obligations or connections. There are multiple texts that show that the baptized faithless are connected to Christ in an important *and very real* sense. This is why it can truly be said that I believe in the objectivity of the covenant. But there is another sense in which such a person does not belong to Christ because he lives in darkness—which is why I am an evangelical.

Branches are cut off the olive tree *for a reason*, and that reason is that they did not have *faith*. The unbelieving Jews were cut off because of unbelief, and we stand by faith, and faith means faith alone, and this is the text I would point to if asked to defend Luther's statement that *sola fidei* is the article of a standing or falling church. It is what the apostle *says*.

So let us devise a thought experiment. If the Last Trump blew tomorrow morning, or if an asteroid landed on a convention center with thousands of Christians in it, or if every professing Christian in North America had a fatal heart attack this evening at 7 p.m., what would happen to all the deceased? Got the picture? We are playing musical chairs, and the music stops. What would happen to those people? My point, and it is a simple one, is that some would be saved and some would be damned.

My point has *nothing whatever to do with the ratios* of those two groups. It is one of life's little ironies that Christians who are clear on the fact that there *are* two such groups are generally muddled on how many of them God has loved with an everlasting love. They are long on logic, but short on love, and therefore bad at math. The theology of this thing is unchanged whether there is one lost individual and ninety-nine saved, or the other way around, or fifty-fifty. If the intervention of God reveals that some were not Christians *indeed*, then that gives us the two categories that are understood by evangelical Christians—some covenant members in good standing are unregenerate and the rest are regenerate, and it doesn't matter how many people are in each respective group in order to have those two groups.

It is no good to grant the whole thing as a hypothetical reality, but then go on to say that who belongs to each group is none of our business. It *is* our business, and the crucial business of every pastor. Examine yourselves, the apostle says, to see if Jesus Christ is in you (2 Cor. 13:5). I quote this verse cheerfully, knowing that it does not mean that we are to be given over to morbid introspection. But having acknowledged that it does not mean that, let us press on to the understanding that it does mean *something*.

It is no good to dismiss the division of sheep and goats as an eschatological vision and thus put it out of all practical consideration. This is because, when it comes to these things, the Bible requires us to count by ones, and it requires us to start with the one closest to home. Suppose the Great Eschaton is ten thousand years off. It remains a stubborn but persistent fact that *my* launch into that Eschaton is no more than fifty years off. It is appointed unto man once to die, and after that the judgment (Heb. 9:27). When the wicked man falls, his hope perishes (Prov. 11:7). The tree lies in the forest right where it falls. Everyone who is over fifty is very certain to discover within fifty or so years whether he or she is a sheep or a goat, wheat or a tare, trusting in Jesus or deluded by the devil. The eschatological scythe harvests every individual long before it harvests the world.

What does it profit a man if he gains the whole world but loses *his own soul* (Matt. 16:26)? The rich fool gloried in his barn-building prowess, not knowing that that very evening his life would be required of him (Luke 12:20). Would things have been any different if he had been glorying in the size of the barns that *God* was going to need (Matt. 13:30)? He would have still been out of it, and his life was still forfeit. This means the way things are going to play out at the Last Day have an extremely personal relevance to every last human being within an error margin of a hundred years, give or take. The long and winding road between now and the Last Day is thousands of miles long, but it is a road down which no living man will be able to kick any cans farther than fifty yards.

And sure, this is a bottom-line, cash-it-out kind of calculus. Some might object that it is too individualistic, and speculate that its influence on us is due to the revivalistic emphasis of the Kentucky frontier. Actually, the reasons Christians keep coming back to this issue of individual salvation is that Jesus used to *say* stuff. Jesus said that to gain the whole world (a corporate category) in exchange for one's *own soul* (kind of individualistic, wouldn't you say?) would be what He, Jesus, would call a bad trade (Matt. 16:26). He said that we should take heed *to ourselves* (Luke 17:3). Do not fear man, but rather the one who can throw body and soul into Hell (Luke 12:5). Now when I fear God, who can throw body and soul into Hell, it is worth asking whose body and whose soul can be so thrown. And the answer is, well, *mine.*

So then, back to the definition of regeneration, which is the new heart that reveals the new Father who has begotten it. I am defining regeneration as an action of God in the soul, whereby He puts to death the old man, such that, if that person were to die, God would own him as a true son, and not deny him. Those who are owned as true sons were regenerate, and those who were denied were not regenerate.

Here is the basic evangelical understanding. There are disciples and there are disciples *indeed* (John 8:31). There are Jews and there are Jews inwardly (Rom. 2:29). Not all Israel are of

Israel (Rom. 9:6). There are Christians who abide in Christ, and Christians who don't (John 15:1–6). There is the outside of the cup, and then there is the inside of it (Matt. 23:26). This means there are Christians and there are Christians *indeed*. We are called to be the latter, not the former, and it is possible to know oneself to be included in the latter group without being given over to morbidity.

A BRIEF HISTORY OF REFORMED EVANGELICALISM

So what is an evangelical? The Greek word for gospel or good news is *evangel*, and so the first and primary meaning of the word should be a reference to someone who accepts the truth of that proclamation. And here at the very beginning of our work we see the conundrum that has necessitated further developments of that word. Someone who believes the truth of that proclamation, or someone who *really* believes it?

The *evangel* is nicely summarized by the Apostles' Creed. This is an objective message, outside ourselves. God, for us men and for our salvation, sent down the Lord Jesus to die for our sins, be buried, and to be raised for our justification. An evangelist is someone who preaches that message, and an evangelical is someone who believes him. But to project our meaning of evangelical back into the early history of the church would be anachronistic. They didn't talk about it that way.

The word *evangelical* began to be used widely as a result of the Lutheran Reformation. In this sense it was simply a term for the Lutherans and referred primarily to the recovery of the objective gospel, the *evangel*. In this sense, it was like the early church—pointing to the realities of the objective gospel—but in this case the word also began to be used to describe those who embraced the recovery of this gospel. There was a great revival of the Spirit going on, but the word was not pointing to anything inside the believer particularly.

Things began to change among the Reformed. As the gulf between Lutherans and Reformed grew, an emphasis on personal regeneration began to grow among the Reformed. In my view, this was the result of the basic disagreement between Reformed and Lutheran on the sacraments. Calvin was closer to Luther than to Zwingli in his view of the Lord's Supper, but closer to Zwingli in what he believed ought to be the basis of ecclesiastical unity. That watershed was, in my view, highly significant, and helped to get us here.

But for whatever reason, an emphasis developed on distinguishing the regenerate from the unregenerate, even within the confines of the Reformed church, or indeed, *especially* within the confines of the Reformed church. It boils down to this. If you can have two baptized men, members in good standing in a good church, both of them communing regularly, and both of them deacons, and one of them has God for his Father, and the other one has the devil for his father, then it is necessary to develop a theological category to process this. The Reformed, at least as far as their confessional standards went, developed this with the language of personal regeneration.

Here are a few examples (emphases added).[14]

The Belgic Confession says this:

> We believe that this *true faith*, produced in man by the hearing of God's Word and by the work of the Holy Spirit, *regenerates him and makes him a 'new man,' causing him* to live the 'new life' and freeing him from the slavery of sin. (Art. 24)

The Heidelberg Catechism, asking whether we are so corrupt as to be incapable of doing any good, replies in this way:

---

14 You can find the complete documents referenced in this chapter online at the Center for Reformed Theology and Apologetics, "Historic Church Documents," http://www.reformed.org/documents/index.html.

Indeed we are . . . *except we are regenerated* by the Spirit of God (Q. 8).

Regeneration addresses the problem of our innate depravity. In questions 71 and 73, the explicit issue of the distinction between regeneration and the laver of regeneration (baptism) comes up. Baptism with water is the promise of cleansing, and the blood and the Spirit actually wash us from our sins, just as the water of baptism washes our bodies.

The Thirty-Nine Articles distinguish the damned from the regenerate (Art. IX), and says that baptism is a "*sign* of regeneration or new birth" (Art. XXVII).

The Irish Articles are quite plain:

All God's elect are *in their time* inseparably united unto Christ *by the effectual and vital influence of the Holy Ghost*, derived from him as from the head unto every true member of his mystical body. And being thus made one with Christ, they are *truly regenerated*, and made partakers of him and all his benefits. (Art. 33)

And because this [one Catholic] Church consisteth of all those, and those alone, which are elected by God unto salvation, *and regenerated by the power of his Spirit, the number of whom is known only unto God himself*: therefore it is called the Catholic or universal, and the Invisible Church. (Art. 68)

The Canons of Dordt are explicit and detailed on this subject.

Moreover, when God carries out this good pleasure in his chosen ones, *or works true conversion in them*, he not only sees to it that the gospel is proclaimed to them outwardly, and enlightens their minds powerfully by the Holy Spirit so that they may rightly understand and discern the things of the Spirit of God, but, *by the effective operation of the same regenerating Spirit*, he also penetrates into the inmost being of man, opens the closed heart, softens the hard heart, and circumcises the heart that is uncircumcised. He infuses new qualities into the will, making the dead will alive, the evil one good, the unwilling one willing, and the stubborn one compliant; he activates and strengthens the will so that, like a good tree, it may be enabled to produce the fruits of good deeds. (Art. 11)

And this is the regeneration, the new creation, the raising from the dead, and the making alive so clearly proclaimed in the Scriptures, which God works in us without our help. But this certainly does not happen only by outward teaching, by moral persuasion, or by such a way of working that, after God has done his work, it remains in man's power whether or not to be reborn or converted. Rather, it is *an entirely supernatural work,* one that is at the same time most powerful and most pleasing, a marvelous, hidden, and inexpressible work, which is not lesser than or inferior in power to that of creation or of raising the dead, as Scripture (inspired by the author of this work) teaches. As a result, *all those in whose hearts God works in this marvelous way are certainly, unfailingly, and effectively reborn and do actually believe.* And then the will, now renewed, is not only activated and motivated by God but in being activated by God is also itself active. For this reason, man himself, by that grace which he has received, is also rightly said to believe and to repent. (Art. 12)

The Westminster Confession is strongest on this subject in the chapter on the effectual call, which is, in effect, another name for the same reality of a regenerating conversion.

They who are *effectually called and regenerated,* having *a new heart and a new spirit created in them,* are further sanctified, really and personally, through the virtue of Christ's death and resurrection, by his Word and Spirit dwelling in them; the dominion of the whole body of sin is destroyed, and the several lusts thereof are more and more weakened and mortified, and they more and more quickened and strengthened, in all saving graces, to the practice of true holiness, without which no man shall see the Lord. (WCF 13.1)

Westminster also openly acknowledges that members of the visible church can be unregenerate:

> Although *hypocrites, and other unregenerate men,* may vainly
> deceive themselves with false hopes and carnal presumptions:
> of being in the favor of God and estate of salvation; which
> hope of theirs shall perish. (WCF 18.1)

Now the Reformed had this emphasis, and it was a pronounced emphasis. But they did not call what they were talking
about *evangelical*—that had to await further developments.

The Reformed emphasis and heritage was overwhelmingly
predominant in the English-speaking world (as distinct
from the Lutheran emphasis), and this lasted for about 150
years, after which there was a great Evangelical Awakening
(there's our word again) in England. It was called the Great
Awakening here. With Whitefield and Wesley leading, the
awakening put a spotlight on the necessity of the new birth,
but the spotlight was on getting people to *experience* it, and
not just affirm it.

Whitefield remained within the Reformed and Calvinistic
heritage, while Wesley veered from it. But both pressed the
absolute necessity of the new birth. The negative result of this
was a disparagement of the institutional church, while the
positive result was that a bunch of people got saved. Over the
next century and a half, the need for personal regeneration
came into high prominence in the revivalistic movements that
swept certain portions of North America, Scotland and Wales.

This revivalistic approach did not overemphasize personal
regeneration; they actually *underemphasized* everything else.
Over time, this evangelical tradition developed its own culture
(although it was largely an ecclesiastical culture), and the last
and best representative of this tradition (in the Whitefieldian
or Edwardian stream of it) was Martyn Lloyd-Jones. In the
Wesleyan stream I would put revivalists like D.L. Moody and
Billy Graham. Ironically, the non-Reformed stream has had a
larger impact on the surrounding culture outside the church

than the Reformed stream of it has, at least in North America, which is one of those weird, go-figure things.

I am a product of this evangelical culture. I am conversant in it and, in some ways, at home in it. But after Jimmy Carter made it okay for everybody to be "born again," North American evangelicalism exploded and became a huge mountain range of cotton candy, and of course, that kind of thing makes me crazy. I have been at war with that stuff for some decades now. But the older, soberer forms of evangelicalism—represented by men like Carl Henry, Lloyd-Jones, or A.W. Tozer—are worthy of our respect, a respect that I *love* to render. They were guarding something that I also want to guard, even as we labor to restore some of the lost reformational emphases—such as the need for a higher view of the church, and a resultant Christendom. I think the world of Lloyd-Jones, but of course, because of a number of things that I am laboring to bring back, I have no reason to think that he would think the world of *me*. I actually think he would look at me with squinty eyes.

I don't want us to be playing evangelical Whac-A-Mole. The earthier aspects of the Reformed faith were whacked for the sake of revivalism. But if we whack "revivalism," and begin to neglect preaching for true and abiding conversion, then we are just going to rebuild the kind of cobwebby Christendom that the next Kirkegaard will have a ball making fun of.

Now I am a minister in the Communion of Reformed Evangelical Churches. What does "Evangelical" mean here? The reference in our name affirms the fundamental need for a new birth for all men, but only *as our respective Reformed confessions articulate it*. I have drawn a connection between our North American forms of evangelicalism and the classic evangelicalism of the Reformed confessions, but it is not "non-evangelical" to disagree with me about that connection. There are any number of ministers in our gathering of churches who do not have the same warm spot in their heart that I do for the two sober clowns remaining in the modern circus of evangelicalism, and that is perfectly okay. But all of us are committed to our classical and confessional expressions of the reality that *our* use of the word *evangelical* points to.

WHAT IS AN EVANGELICAL?

IN HIS SMALL BOOK *What Is An Evangelical?* Martyn Lloyd-Jones says a number of helpful things (along with some pretty unhelpful ones). But one of the helpful ones was this—"The next thing, clearly, about the evangelical is *the tremendous emphasis that he puts upon the rebirth. This is absolutely basic to him . . . .*"[15]

But before proceeding farther, it is necessary to head off misunderstandings. An evangelical is someone who emphasizes, as Lloyd-Jones puts it, the absolute necessity of the new birth. But doing this doesn't mean that *he* is born again. The Spirit moves as he wills, and not when we snap our fingers, proclaiming the right formulae. Being born again is not the same thing as *saying*, "You must be born again." And flipped around, there are saints who do not maintain or emphasize the doctrine of the new birth as I am arguing they ought to—but who are godly, fruitful saints nonetheless. There are plenty of born again people who wouldn't call it that, and there are plenty of evangelicals who need to get saved. Life is messy.

Speaking on a personal note, much of my Christian life has been shaped and formed by godly teachers that I would not describe as evangelicals. The patron saint of this weird set up

---

15 Martyn Lloyd-Jones, *What Is An Evangelical?* (Carlisle, PA: Banner of Truth, 1993), 56.

would be C.S. Lewis. He was not an evangelical, but his godliness and insight have been a major contributor in making me a better Christian . . . and a better evangelical.

Another way of putting this could be fun. Let us speak of visible evangelicalism and invisible evangelicalism. Visible evangelicalism is a set of doctrinal commitments and priorities. I am arguing for the importance of those things, especially as a set of strategic commitments for preachers, which I will explain a bit more farther down.

I have also described myself as a catholic evangelical, not a sectarian one. This means that the boundaries of my fellowship extend beyond what I believe to be important for me to emphasize in my preaching and writing.

In the realm of the visible church, and using some shorthand, I would define a Christian as one who is committed to the truths found in the Apostles' Creed. I would define a Reformed Christian as one who is committed to the five *solas*—*sola Scriptura*, *sola gratia*, *sola fide*, *solus Christus*, and *soli Deo gloria*. An evangelical is one who emphasizes a strict biblicism, an activist spirit, and a crucicentric proclamation of the gospel resulting in the new birth. You can see at a glance that most of this last definition is found in the Reformation tradition, with the one exception of emphasizing the new birth. And *that* was emphasized in certain quarters during the Reformation era also, but not across the board.

So why go on about this? What's the importance of it? What's the big deal? I am arguing this way as a *pastor*, as a shepherd of souls, as a preacher. I want my people to get their doctrine right, of course, just as I want them to get their worship right, and so on. But fundamentally, I want them to go to Heaven with me. This is the goal of all ministry.

"Whom we preach, *warning every man*, and teaching every man in all wisdom; *that we may present every man perfect in Christ Jesus*" (Col. 1:28).

As we have been engaged in the work of establishing our congregation here, over the years I have seen very clearly the ability that (not a few) professing Christians have to be attracted to a work just like ours, to join with us, to check the doctrinal and liturgical boxes, to present their babies for baptism, to come to worship regularly, and yet to live in ways (in private and openly within their families) that the Bible describes as utterly inconsistent with inheriting the kingdom of Heaven. And we must speak about this as the Bible does, when there is biblical warrant for doing so.

> Know ye not that *the unrighteous shall not inherit the kingdom of God?* Be not deceived: neither fornicators, nor idolaters, nor adulterers, nor effeminate, nor abusers of themselves with mankind, nor thieves, nor covetous, nor drunkards, nor revilers, nor extortioners, *shall inherit the kingdom of God.* (1 Cor. 6:9–10)

> Now the works of the flesh are manifest, which are these; Adultery, fornication, uncleanness, lasciviousness, idolatry, witchcraft, hatred, variance, emulations, wrath, strife, seditions, heresies, envyings, murders, drunkenness, revellings, and such like: of the which I tell you before, as I have also told you in time past, *that they which do such things shall not inherit the kingdom of God.* (Gal. 5:19–21)

> For this ye know, that no whoremonger, nor unclean person, nor covetous man, who is an idolater, *hath any inheritance in the kingdom of Christ and of God.* (Eph. 5:5)

So how is a pastor to get *at* that stuff? I don't know any other way to be a pastor to such people than to insist, repeatedly, on the necessity of the new birth. If they were regenerate, they wouldn't be living like that. Everything else we might ask them to do, they have done—and yet the anger continues, the porn use continues, the drunkenness continues, the sorrow that leads only to death continues. If such a person says, defiantly, that he will not quit whatever it is, then of course the problem is solved through church discipline. That's what church discipline is for.

But what if such a person professes repentance every time (Luke 17:4)? At a certain point, a wise pastor has to raise the possibility that what this parishioner really needs to do is "get saved." But in order to do *that*, there has to be a theological framework for it. You don't want a pornmeister blinking at you uncomprehendingly. "But I *am* saved. You baptized me."

As any experienced pastor can tell you, this is not a hypothetical problem. This is life in the visible church, and I really think our discussions of clerical garb should always start with the muck boots.

CATHOLIC EVANGELICALISM

WITH THIS BOOK DEDICATED TO DEFENDING the absolute necessity of the new birth, one question that might arise is this—who or what am I arguing with? Why is such a book necessary? Here is a quick answer, or at least as quick as a fourfold answer can be.

First, as Chesterton noticed, when Satan fell, he fell by the force of gravity. We sin, when we sin, downhill. The fact that God has introduced the new creation into this world, the new humanity, does not keep Heaven from being up, and up means uphill. This does not in any way nullify the reality and all-pervasiveness of grace, but it rather means, simply, that grace is what enables us to want to walk uphill. When we get tired of walking uphill, this is another way of saying that we are getting tired of His grace. Grace does what it does, and not something else.

But sinners love affirming the consequent, and so they think that this somehow means that anything difficult (anything uphill-like) must be, on this definition, some form of grace. And thus it is that many stair-steppers for a works mentality are manufactured, and one is installed in the family room of the religionist, so that he can have *all* the sweat and be no closer to glory when he is done.

So the first reason for emphasizing the new birth is that this is the only antidote to the carnal mind, and the carnal mind is a downhill mind. The natural man does not discern the things of the Spirit, because they are spiritually discerned (1 Cor. 2:14). Grace only makes sense to a gracious mind, and so this is why I emphasize the new birth. In this world, the saints I am responsible for pastoring are confronted daily with an awful lot of downhill options. If we are to take up the cross daily, and we are (Luke 9:23), the purpose of every cross is a resurrection. This is why we may walk in newness of life (Rom. 6:4). Walking in newness of life means walking in the regeneration.

The second reason is that I am part of a larger effort to reform the worship of the church. Liturgical reformation is most necessary, for reasons I have argued for elsewhere, but emphasizing the objectivity of worship and the sacraments, and the spiritual reality of the visible church, brings its own set of temptations. This is not an argument against such a reformation, any more than math problems are an argument against math classes, but those who try to recruit people into math classes by ignorantly or dishonestly ignoring the immediate presence of math problems are not helping matters at all.

Without regeneration, the most glorious church service ever conducted is rank superstition, and God hates it. When the life goes out of worship, it is not long after that the (few remaining) living go out too. Those in whom the new life still resides will not wait around too long in a mausoleum. Over the last few centuries, the mass exodus of evangelicals from the formal, liturgical churches was, by and large, well justified. It was good that they were chased out, and it was good that the others left. We might be accused of leaving the one, holy, catholic, and apostolic church, and if we are accused of this, we might reply that the marble floors, the guttering candles, and all the dead bodies had started to creep us out.

If I want to help lead evangelicals back to more respectful worship, *and I do*, one of the things I must do is demonstrate for them that I understand what drove them out in the first place. Worship God in a decorated palace tomb without the Spirit? I'd rather go to Hell, but I repeat myself. Hell is any place where God has withdrawn His favor. Anybody who wants to lead the saints into a more formal worship had better ensure that it is a formal *and lively* worship. And by lively I do not mean having a preacher who waves his arms while speaking—I mean a community that has experienced, and walks in, the new birth. Anything else can go to blazes.

It was entirely predictable, but in this nascent movement back to God-honoring worship, worship that is characterized by the reverent awe that the Scriptures require (Heb. 12:28–29), a contingent of voices has arisen, not to reassure evangelicals that such worship need not be as dead as a six-ton slab of cold marble, but rather to demonstrate just how cold that marble can be. But look how it *shines*!

Third, in a different direction, there are some who object to the doctrine of the new birth on philosophical grounds. They wonder if we have such a thing as a "nature" that admits of an ontological change into another kind of nature. Those who read through the issue of *Credenda/Agenda* on the Federal Vision saw "A Joint Federal Vision Profession," the statement that laid out our definition of what we believed the basic issues were. At the conclusion of that statement was a list of issues on which FV participants differ among themselves, and "whether regeneration represents a change of nature" was one of those issues.[16] What this means is that some FV advocates are evangelicals (in the sense of affirming the necessity of the new birth) and some are not. This does not mean that I accuse those who differ with me on this subject of heresy—it simply means that I would say they are not evangelicals in this specified sense. There are many fine Christians who have not been

---

16   John Barach, et al., "A Joint Federal Vision Profession," *Credenda/Agenda* 19.3 (Special Edition 2007): 13.

evangelicals, so this is not an attempt at a slam. But I *am* an evangelical, and I believe that historic evangelicalism (as distinguished from what has become a pink-bubblegum form of evangelicalism) has contributed something important to the general inheritance of the catholic church. We brought a gift for the treasury, and I don't want to see it sold off in the annual rummage sale. I write as a *catholic* evangelical, not a sectarian one, but I still want our evangelical center to hold.

And last, the new birth is important to emphasize because we live in postmodern times, and blurred distinctions are a natural refuge for those who want to hide from God. This is why the unregenerate love postmodernism so much. But as one Puritan put it, we serve a *precise* God, which is gloriously true. The holiness code taught the Israelites their ABCs—this, not that, here, not there. If the accident happens on this side of the border, you will be tried in this jurisdiction, and six inches over, you will be tried in that one. Male and female created He them. A fertilized human egg will live forever, and an unfertilized one won't. God draws razor lines between soul and spirit, and between bones and marrow. The living God is the God who distinguishes, and sinners need to deal with it.

So then, if it is true that certain members of the covenant, as baptized as anybody around here, can die and go to Hell, then there must be something which distinguishes them from those who do not. The Bible describes this distinction, over and over again, as a matter of regeneration. Sons of the devil (with all their sacramental papers in order nonetheless) were his sons by generation. They cannot become sons of another without *another* generation, without a regeneration. Here is the great question that every living soul must be confronted with at some point, and which preachers are charged to deliver to them—who's your daddy?

One of the great issues that Federal Vision advocates fought for was *the right to speak as the Bible speaks*. But this is more than double-bladed—this is a regular Swiss army knife. Not only do we speak biblically when we call the baptismal font the laver of regeneration (which it certainly is), we also speak biblically when we say of multitudes who have been presented at that very same font, that they are vipers, sons of the devil, unwashed pigs, whitewashed tombs, blind guides, tares planted by an enemy, unfruitful branches, and clouds without rain—in short, unregenerate.

And what do these unregenerate need? They need Jesus, of course, but Jesus is received by evangelical faith alone. And to round this circle out, I am not calling these religionists away from the church—I am inviting them *in*. They are the ones knocking about on the outside of the sacraments, the outside of worship, the outside of the psalms, the outside of the kingdom. As the great Puritan Thomas Watson put it, not everyone who hangs around the court speaks with the king.

APOSTASY AND THE NEW BIRTH

ONE OF THE REASONS why we talk past each other on the question of apostasy is that we succumb to the common mistake of choosing which verses are the "clear" ones. A hermeneutical rule of thumb (and quite a good one, I should add) is that unclear verses should be interpreted in the light of the clear ones. But however wise this is—and it *is* wise—we also have to distinguish between verses which are unclear, and verses that are excruciatingly clear but which conflict with the received interpretation.

It is this latter situation which causes Christians to arbitrarily dub *these* as the clear verses and those *other* verses as the ones that must be massaged. On this question of apostasy, both Calvinists and Arminians do this. Calvinists take the verses outlining God's sovereignty in salvation at face value (which they should do) and explain away the apostasy passages. Arminians take the apostasy passages at face value and explain away the glorious promises of a guaranteed perseverance. Thought experiment: What would happen if you took them *all* at face value? You would get in trouble with *everybody*, like the guy at Gettysburg who tried to make peace by walking in between the armies with a blue coat and gray trousers.

The Bible emphasizes, through some of its illustrations, a certain continuity of type between the converted and unconverted covenant member. In the parable of the sower, the converted and unconverted both spring from the same seed, and they are both wheat. The Bible emphasizes, in other illustrations, a radical discontinuity of type between the two—a sow that is washed is always a sow. Tares are not wheat—they are an alien plant, likely darnel, in the wheat field. We should take *both* kinds of illustration at face value. In one respect, there is a radical gulf between converted and unconverted covenant members, a gulf as wide as the distance between Heaven and Hell. In another respect, there is a shared covenantal identity of some sort. Fruitful and fruitless branches are found in the Vine, although the fruitless ones are not found there for long. Fruitful and fruitless branches are found in the olive tree of the true Israel—although the only way to remain in that tree is by having the faith of Abraham.

So much is a statement of the problem. What is the solution to the problem? How can we take both kinds of passages at face value? There is only one way—and that is by emphasizing, in its right biblical balance, *the absolute necessity of the new birth* for every last human being, not excluding those who are baptized Christians.

Even in the parable of the sower, note how Jesus explains the difference between different kinds of wheat. The wheat in rocky soil sprang up quickly. It sprang up from the seed that was sown. It was wheat, but it was wheat that died, wheat that did not persevere to the harvest. And why? Jesus says that it was because that man had "no root in himself" (*ouk rhitzan en auto*). This wheat did not have *within itself* something that the abundant wheat did have (Matt. 13:21). You must be converted to God.

Jesus told a teacher in Israel once that he needed to be born again. Israel today, the new Israel, is filled to overflowing with that same kind of teacher, the kind that ought to know better.

So it cannot be the case that all who are covenantally "in Christ" by virtue of baptism are in exactly the same position as regards the grace and favor of God—with no distinction save that some persevere somehow. To think that having "all grace" except for persevering grace is somehow reassuring is to have a wildly skewed sense of priorities. "Other than that, how was the play, Mrs. Lincoln?" How is God's withholding of perseverance not a refusal of grace? If we say that the grace was forfeited by those who subjectively resisted His work in their lives "too much," then why did God withhold from them the gift of "not resisting too much?"

There is clearly a connection between the Ten Commandments and Ezekiel's description of hearts of stone—this appears to be a connection the apostle Paul makes, also. But this does not really weaken the need for individual regeneration. How could it? The apostolic treatment concludes with an indictment of individual covenant members. "But their minds were blinded: for until this day remaineth the same vail untaken away in the reading of the old testament; which vail is done away in Christ. But even unto this day, when Moses is read, the vail is upon their heart" (2 Cor. 3:14–15).

Blindness is a condition which covenant members then and now can certainly have. If the change in a person is simply relational, then how can these covenant members be described as blinded and having a veil on their hearts? Relationally, they would have to be identical to the elect.

Some may want to talk about passages like this one, or the wheat and tares, and ignore the passages like John 15. But we don't want to be guilty of the reverse problem, camping out in John 15 and failing to treat the fact that many of the illustrations indicate an ontological difference between the elect and reprobate within the covenant as one existing *the entire time.* Tares are weeds the entire time, the sow that is washed is a clean pig but still has a natural affinity for the mire, the dog that vomited is still a dog. On the other side, all the branches are true branches, including those to be cut out, etc. We should

simply want to affirm all the passages at face value and to let
God sort it out. The only way I can do this is affirm the objectivity of the covenant, affirm that ontological differences exist
between the elect and the reprobate whether the covenant is
involved or not, and affirm that we should not pry too closely
into it. We should preach and declare that these things are so,
not that we know what and where and how they are so.

I want to affirm this kind of ontological anthropology
because the Bible repeatedly does, but it does so in terms of
the nature of the ancestry. It speaks of thorn bushes, vipers, the
devil's children, and so on, and it does this frequently when
addressing those covenant members whose spiritual ancestry
(and therefore nature) ought to have been different than it was.

If we understand this, we can understand the promises of God
that were given to us as a *guarantee* of our future inheritance.
In the biblical approach, God comes *down*. He came down in
the Incarnation, and He comes down when He descends into
our lives and hearts. He gives *Himself* to us as a guarantee (2
Cor. 1:22; Eph. 1:14). One of the things we should not want to
find ourselves doing is to affirm that God is like that manufacturer who issues a "lifetime guarantee" for His products, and
then when it breaks and you take it in, you discover that the
guarantee was for the lifetime of the *product*, which apparently
ended at the very moment it broke. The Spirit-given guarantee
needs to do something—it needs to *guarantee*.

If two customers take their warranty back to the factory, and
their circumstances are identical (the product broke), and one
has the warranty honored and the other does not, there are only
two real possibilities. One is that the manufacturer is a cheat, and
the other is that the customer who was turned away is a cheat.

Those are the options. What is it that voids the warranty?
Where is it? All Christians agree that the problem is on the customer's end, not on God's end. Let God be true, and every man

a liar. But what are the possible problems on man's end?—there are only two. The first is the presence of sin, and the second is the absence of living faith. If the former, then every Christian is going to Hell. If the latter, then we find we have worked our way back to the classic understanding of regeneration.

A BRIEF DEFENSE OF WARFIELD

"Instead of the Church and the sacraments, the means of grace, being conceived, as they are represented in the Scriptures, and as they must be thought of in all healthful religious conceptions of them, as instrumentalities which the Holy Spirit uses in working salvation, the Holy Spirit is made an instrument which the Church, the means of grace, use in working salvation."[17]

Instrumentalities which the Holy Spirit uses in working salvation. Keep that in mind.

One of central themes of Warfield's book *The Plan of Salvation* is the idea that the *sine qua non* of evangelical religion is the doctrine of God's immediate work in salvation. But what exactly is meant by "immediate"? It should be obvious that for Warfield it does not mean an utter absence of mediating means.

It is tempting to think that Warfield means "apart from any instruments or means of grace," but what he actually means is "in hierarchical distinction from any instruments or means of grace." And not surprisingly, this word "distinction" all goes back to the effectual call.

As Warfield notes above, when the Holy Spirit is "working salvation," He is using "instrumentalities." But those instrumentalities *by themselves* are impotent in the work of salvation.

---

17   B. B. Warfield, *The Plan of Salvation* (Lindenhurst, NY: Great Christian Books, 2013), 63.

They mean what they mean, but they do not do what they mean *by themselves*. When the surgeon is gone from the hospital, his instruments are lined up in the drawer, full of potential.

As an aside, I am happy to notice that Warfield avoids the dodge that many contemporary evangelical Presbyterians resort to, which is to insist that salvation has to be the work of an invisible Holy Ghost thunderbolt, while the sacraments are means of sanctifying grace only, never saving grace. But Warfield talks the way the Confession talks, speaking of sacraments and salvation easily and in the same breath.

Nevertheless, his take on what the evangelical stance should be is a sound one. The issue is the immediacy of God's work, but we have to be careful not to misunderstand it. There is a definition of immediacy *apart from* means that would be much closer to some sort of Quaker quietism, or more to the point, closer to a pop evangelical Jesus-in-your-heart, bypass-the-church view than to the understanding of the magisterial reformers. But there is another understanding of immediacy—the effectual call—that is historic and confessional evangelicalism. That is what I am seeking to articulate and defend.

So how can the Holy Spirit use an *instrument* for salvation, and at the same time have the work of salvation be *immediate*? Doesn't the Spirit's use of the instrument at all make His work mediated? No, not in the way that Warfield intends.

The immediacy has to do with God's intention, made manifest by and through the effectual call, the gift of life. That immediate call can take place in a sermon, while reading a book, in the midst of a baptism, or while listening to a street preacher. Place two men, side by side in each instance, with one of them being saved and the other not. The distinction between them is not to be found in the presence and absence of the means, for both of them experienced the same means—whether sermon or sacrament or something else. The distinction between them is found in the efficacy of the means. That power, the authority, the efficacy, is immediate. The means is dependent on the presence of God's power. God's power is not dependent on the presence of the means.

So the other understanding of "immediate" is something which I believe that Warfield, being a good churchman, would reject. That understanding says that if salvation is "immediate," then means are superfluous, and at worst, a hindrance. Some people do try to go in this direction, but since we live in a universe chock full of matter, this is hard to do, as in, impossible to do. They usually just succeed in privileging one means over another one, making *their* use of it invisible to themselves, and then taunting people who picked a different favorite means, a means visible to them. To claim the Holy Spirit can use baptismal water is apparently superstition, but the use of Bibles and sermons is not—even though material means are equally involved in both.

When the Spirit anoints something, *that* makes it effectual, and the effect is immediate. The Spirit's work does not come through the means (the sermon, the sacrament) like water through a garden hose. Rather, the Spirit's anointing is given on account of the means. He is not doing an "end run" around the means. God could easily do it entirely apart from the means, but He chooses not to. He meets us where He promised He would, in the Word and in the sacrament. But if we show up later with our tiny cages in order to capture those very same means, hoping to chain the Spirit up, we find that He is gone.

When the glory departs, the things that were previously glorified are commonly still there. When God "gives the increase," this is something that only God can do. When He does this, it is immediate. When God gives life—and He is the life-giver—it is immediate.

The mediating means are still present when a man is alive, but they are also all there when he is dead. So the means aren't the thing essential. Adam's body was *there* before the Lord God breathed into him. And when He did, something *else* was there. And that "something else" is what confessional evangelicalism is concerned to protect. This is why Warfield still has an important point to make for us.

The problem is the perennial Jacob and Esau problem, since both those gentlemen were equally circumcised, and both came from the same womb at (almost) the same time. It would be difficult to find a sacramental distinction between them. Their access to the mediated means was equal—which is how Paul uses it in his argument. "Not of works, but of him that calleth" (Rom. 9:11). The distinction between the two was the love of God for Jacob and the hatred of God for Esau—the distinction was in God's intention, and God's *intention* is not mediated. The intention drives the mediation, not the other way around. So, despite the fact that the available means of grace for the two men was identical, one was accepted and the other rejected. And, if anything, Esau's sacramental argument would have been the stronger.

If two men, one saved and one damned, can enjoy the same access to the same means, then the thing which distinguishes them is the faith of the one and the unbelief of the other. But that faith is itself a gift, and it is given in accordance with His sovereign will. The fact that the gift of faith is not inexorably given with every instance of a sacramental gift is what sets up the problem for us, and which is what makes historical evangelicalism a necessity.

Whenever God uses an instrument of grace, then that grace is of course mediated (in that sense, on that level). But when God is using the very same instrument of grace on a reprobate covenant member not three feet away from the first one, there must be a difference (unmediated in *some* sense) in God's intention or in His sovereign decree.

Paul calls this as God "giving the increase." God is the Author of life, and His immediate gift of life is essential. A dead body and a living one both have access to the same organs and limbs, but with one crucial difference. When He determines to give this life, in the Bible it is described in comparison to the one great act that all of us must grant to have been unmediated— the act of creation itself. If anyone is in Christ, he is a new *creation* (2 Cor. 5:17). Or, as Paul argues elsewhere, neither the presence of the sacrament, nor the absence of it, but rather a new *creation* (Gal. 6:15).

The verse that is inscribed on my mother's gravestone points to just this truth. "For God, who commanded the light to shine out of darkness, hath shined in our hearts, to give the light of the knowledge of the glory of God in the face of Jesus Christ" (2 Cor. 4:6).

I am arguing that this command, this intention, *has* to be unmediated. When God commands the light to shine, the heart is consequently lit up. When someone remains in darkness, even if he has laid hold of every sacrament known to man, if he claims to be in the light (while hating his brother, say), the truth is not in him any more than the light is (1 John 1:6).

In short, we should cheerfully grant that God uses instruments and means ordinarily, but I want to argue (and I think that Warfield would agree) that for the converted, there must be an *extra* that is not anchored to anything in this world. It is the evangelical extra, the Warfieldian extra.

A TESTIMONY

I GREW UP IN THE CONTEXT of North American evangelical-ism, which includes two things that are pertinent to this dis-cussion. One is the central emphasis on the new birth, and the other is a host of cultural trappings that developed around that emphasis. I grew up in what might be called cultural evangel-icalism, but in a home that emphasized the nature and *reality* of the new birth (a reality that also characterizes historical and confessional evangelicalism).

After I became Reformed I found myself gradually estranged from many aspects of cultural evangelicalism, ambivalent about some of it, affectionate toward the remainder, but still conversant with all of it. Because of this history, whenever I start emphasiz-ing the importance of something called "evangelicalism," I think that some people believe that my roots are calling me home, or that I somehow want Reformed Christians who have never darkened the doors of a Jesus junk store to head down there now to get themselves some Testamints®. As St. Paul said, when-ever he was accused of this very same thing, *me genoito*!

One of the reasons that I was able to grow out of that par-ticular expression of the faith was the recognition that the historic and confessional expressions of the Reformed faith articulated and expressed the evangelical center I held dear much more capably than the cultural evangelicalism around me did. I stayed faithful to my heritage of evangelicalism, even as I grew out of it.

Heart conversion is an absolute necessity if a sinful man is ever to see a holy God. But conversionism is not any such thing. Conversionism is a set of cultural expressions that grew up around a particular set of the Holy Spirit's movements in history. But those cultural expressions are not absolute. No human cultural expressions ever are. But the Word of God is absolute, and the Spirit's work in the hearts of sinful men never, ever changes. The transformation of life to death is unmistakably the same kind of thing, from Adam to the last sinner in.

So the only thing I am pressing for is a warm embrace of confessional evangelicalism, which teaches the necessity of heart conversion. It does not teach "conversionism." I am not even pressing for anybody who holds to it to call it evangelicalism. In our circles, the doctrine of the effectual call contains everything I want to represent and stand for on this issue. You can tell this from the italics below, which are mine.

> All those whom God hath predestinated unto life, and those only, He is pleased, in His appointed time, *effectually to call*, by His Word and Spirit, *out of that state* of sin and death, in which they are *by nature* to grace and salvation, by Jesus Christ; *enlightening* their minds spiritually and savingly to understand the things of God, *taking away their heart of stone*, and giving unto them an heart of flesh; *renewing their wills*, and, by His almighty power, determining them to that which is good, and effectually drawing them to Jesus Christ: yet so, as they come most freely, being made willing by His grace.[18]

Other covenant members are not effectually called in this same way.

"Others, not elected, although they may be called by the ministry of the Word, and may have some common operations

---

18   *The Westminster Confession of Faith*, 10.1.

of the Spirit, *yet they never truly come unto Christ*, and therefore cannot be saved."[19]

So there is a true coming to Christ, brought about by this effectual call, which is a change of nature, a giving of a heart of flesh for a heart of stone, a renewal of the will, a transfer out of a state of sin and death into a state of enlightenment, and this is all the evangelicalism anybody needs.

So if the Testamints® thing was bugging you, as the Australians say, no worries.

---

19 *The Westminster Confession of Faith*, 10.4.

EPILOGUE

BREAK, BLOW, BURN

IT IS BAD WHEN A WRITER GETS IN OVER HIS HEAD, or when a theologian does, or when a pamphleteer does, or when a connector-of-the-dots does. But, with all necessary qualifications made, it not bad when a preacher does. It is a preacher's calling to get in over his head (2 Cor. 2:16). But he needs to be careful to do it the right way—there is a way to be in over your head in the pulpit which is just ordinary confusion, and there is a way that is the work of the Spirit of God.

We may look forward to the reunion of all Christendom, and we should do so because it is going to be glorious. But precisely because it is going to be glorious, it will not be the result of careful negotiations hammered out by the canon lawyers. As Lloyd-Jones once memorably put it, getting all the ecclesiastical corpses into one graveyard will not bring about a resurrection.

As a pamphleteer, as a writer, I do find it necessary to argue for the absolute necessity of the new birth, as I have done throughout the course of this book. But for a preacher, much more than this is involved. The preacher declares words calculated to raise the dead, which is quite different than flattering the living. When the Spirit is pleased to move, He will do so.

But the Spirit, when He moves, will not be like a little zephyr, stirring the gauzy curtains of our theological library. His moving will be more like a massive thunderhead, silver on the top and utterly black on the bottom, coming in from the west, and looking to soak absolutely everybody.

I am an evangelical, the son of evangelicals, and so I do insist on the absolute necessity of the new birth. That's our wineskin. There is nothing wrong with wineskins, because wine always has to go into something. But there is something wrong with empty wineskins, and there is something wrong with the idea that trafficking in the idea of wine is the same thing as the wine itself, which it isn't.

The glories that are coming will be the result of *what* we are talking about and not the result *of* our talking about it. Elegant formulations are necessary in their way, but they are also as dead as an idiom about doornails. Reformation and revival consists of the reality of the Spirit moving, and we cannot whistle Him up—we can't do it with sacraments, we can't do it with church music, and we can't do by rolling up our shirt sleeves in order to preach a hot gospel. Here, hold your mouth *this* way, and maybe that will make the Spirit fall.

But the Spirit will fall. The thunderhead will roll in. And when it happens, the work of regeneration will be a gully washer, and lots of ecclesiastics will be pretty upset. But many more of them will be soaked through, and it will become increasingly harder to preach our little floating dust cloud sermons.

And it will not be preaching that ushers this in, but rather the *folly* of preaching. But mark it well—the Spirit never moves in such a way as to leave things right where He found them. The detritus of religiosity—whether prohibited by Scripture or required by it—will be either washed away or washed clean. I speak of icons, candles, sermon manuscripts, choral anthems, lectionaries, processionals, and white eucharistic table cloths.

If you want it all to be washed clean, and not washed away, then fasten it to the plain teaching of Scriptures with the nails of evangelical faith and use as many of them as you have.

When God pleases, and He showers us with kindness, we will be given the wisdom found in the old song "God Don't Never Change":

> God in the pulpit,
> God way back at the door,
> God in the amen corner,
> God all over the floor

So let us try to forget the word *evangelical* as a demographic description. Let us try to forget the word *liturgical* as a description of the boring church you grew up in. Let us try to forget the word *doctrine* as it was handled by that great nineteenth-century divine, the Rev. Dr. Snodgood, in three volumes.

When the fire falls, all of these things are glorious. When the glory departs, all of them are Ichabodian. It makes no sense to argue for the glory of the house after it has been left to us desolate.

When a certain doctrinal controversy broke out a few years ago, it was necessary to take the fire hose of grace to the doctrinal gnat-stranglers. But we have to always remember that—in *Scripture*—the fire hose of grace sprays in a 360-degree radius, and not just 180, where those *other* guys are standing. *We* can get soaked pretty good too, and those standing with and near us the same.

The world is suffused with the glory of God; the world is sacramental. And when our sin causes Jesus to break fellowship with the rebellion, it is a dead sacrament to the rebels. What can we make dead by this means? Actually, what *can't* we make dead? Doctrine, liturgy, processionals, cantatas, plans of salvation, gospel-as-story, you name it.

If we are to be faithful servants, *we must speak the way the Bible speaks*. We must attack what the Bible attacks, and defend what the Bible defends. If we do this, we must be prepared to be accused of being "unbalanced" and "unfair." But as Peter Leithart wonderfully began *Against Christianity*, "I have written an unbalanced book. I have written an unfair book. I have written a fragmented book." Amen, and let us have much more of it. And why?

If we are unbalanced, we might one day fall over into glory. If we are unfair, we might find that we are actually being unfair to all the hidden cheat codes of our unctuous religiosity. Forgiveness, after all, is pretty unfair. If we learn to scatter more fragments of grace, a second glance might reveal them all to have become diamonds the moment they left our hands.

Aslan is not a tame lion. Shift used that truth destructively, and to his own damnation, but it was still a truth for all that. We don't care that God's grace is not domesticated, and cannot be domesticated. We don't care that God is not tame. He's *good*, I tell you.

Think for a minute. Donne's "Holy Sonnet 14" has some wisdom for us. You want your worship and your devotion to spring up like a well? You want to be made new, you say? It cannot happen unless we invite Him to "break, blow, burn." That line ends with "make me new."

And may the Spirit help us to know what we ask for.

APPENDIX

BITING THE LEFT HIND LEG

Some may be wondering why I have been on this regeneration jag. Well, in the first place, jags are how I operate. That's just how I roll. Some others may wonder how this "jag," as I put it, relates to the positions I took in the Federal Vision controversy some years ago. Here are some thoughts on that.

1. *"Reformed" Is Not Enough* (henceforth *RINE*) was published in 2002, eleven years ago.[20] What I have written in this book does not represent in any way a "walking back" of what I argued there. Rather, it is a straightforward application of it. More about that in a moment. Right now, let me note that the ground is not shifting under our feet. This is what I said then:

    > We see in this portion of the Confession that a man is "quickened and renewed" in such a way as to enable him to respond to the call of God. This might be called regeneration, theologically considered. A man is either regenerate or he is not. When the word regeneration is being used in this sense, we are talking about an individual operation performed by

---

20   Douglas Wilson, *"Reformed" Is Not Enough: Recovering the Objectivity of the Covenant* (Moscow, ID: Canon Press, 2002).

the Spirit of God, who does what He does when and how it pleases Him. And when we are talking about what might be called this "effectual call-regeneration," we have to repudiate every form of baptismal or decisional regeneration. (p. 39)

This is from a chapter which argues at length that the objectivity of the covenant is not in any way inconsistent with evangelicalism, classically understood. Later on, there is a chapter on assurance of salvation (chapter 14), in which I work through the scriptural evidences by which a covenant member is invited to conclude that he has the root of the matter in him. Then there are three chapters on the Christians who aren't Christians—on heretics (chapter 16), on sons of Belial (chapter 17), and on false brothers (chapter 18). Baked into this cake was my assumption that covenant members are either regenerate or they are not (p. 34).

2.   But why this jag more than a decade after? My son Nate recently observed that a good border collie does not just decide (for the sake of doctrinal consistency) that he will always nip at a sheep's left hind leg. He alternates, and does so with a larger purpose in view.

A good shepherd of the Lord's flock does the same sort of thing. The issue is not what you would put down on paper as a systematic expression of all your views—you have to talk, preach, write, blog, and write books, in terms of where the flock is actually going, and where it needs to be going.

When it comes to these sorts of issues, a pastor in our circles has to be concerned about two things—"respectable" defections from the Reformed tradition and disreputable collapses into horrendous sin. For the former, I have in mind things like conversions to Rome or Eastern Orthodoxy, problems like that. Moves like that come from somewhere, and so maybe it is time to nip at the right hind legs.

For the latter I have in mind parishioners who are rolling around in Galatians 5:19–21 with shouts of libertine joy. It is time to attack this kind of covenantal presumption, and it needs to be attacked with a canoe paddle. I wish I could say this is a hypothetical problem, but it has not been. I have a greater responsibility to be attacking the linchpin of the devil's system, which is sin, than I have to be defending what I thought was the linchpin of my own system.

In the epilogue to *RINE*, I exhorted everyone to fight sin within these categories.

> We vary between two extremes. The first extreme is to say that people who are guilty of such things are not Christians at all, in any sense, and so we rid the body of Christ of them. Unfortunately, by doing this, we also have lost the very concept of a visible body of Christ. We find ourselves saying that a man who has never met Christ has betrayed Him. In other words, we say that all adulterers were never really married. But of course this means that they are not really adulterers. The other extreme acknowledges that they are in fact Christians, and indeed, let the ecumenical games begin! But this is just as silly. This position is to maintain that if someone is a husband, then adultery is impossible, and we can only speak encouragingly to one another. (p. 195)

I follow it up on the next page with this: "In other words, we have two positions: the first is that husbands cannot commit adultery, and the second is that adulterers are not husbands, and hence not adulterers. What never seems to occur to anyone is the duty of fighting our fellow Christians to the last ditch" (p. 196).

3. One of the great points that advocates of the Federal Vision fought for was the right to speak biblically to God's people, without having that pronouncement instantly disallowed for the sake of a definition from our systematic theology. We did not want to set aside the Word of God for the sake

of our traditions. For example, the Bible obviously teaches the doctrine of decretal election, but not every use of "election" in the Bible follows that usage. I can plead with my people "as the elect of God, to put on tender mercies," and I can do this without affirming that everybody in our church directory is decretally elect. We should talk the way the Bible talks anyway.

But both ends of this teeter-totter go up and down. Do we really think that the "truly reformed" (the TRs) are the only ones with a system? Do we really think that they are the only ones who might be tempted to rush in when biblical language is used in an attempt to save their system? The TR is tempted, when Jesus warns about branches being cut out of the vine, to explain to the faithful that such a branch couldn't really have been a branch and had to have been a bit of tumbleweed or something caught there. He is saving his system, but at the expense of faithfulness to the text. But what happens when a baptized covenant member is stinking up the whole sanctuary, and a pastor says to him that he is a goat, a tare, a cloud without rain, a dog returning to vomit, a pig returning to its sty, and so forth? All of that is biblical language also, addressed in various settings to baptized saints. Special pleading for the sake of a sacramental system is no better than special pleading for another kind of system. We should talk the way the Bible talks anyway.

And of course, we must add the caveat that we should use such biblical language on biblical occasions. It would be inappropriate to exhort a congregation "as the elect of God, to put on tender mercies" right after they voted to call a lesbian minister. And it would be inappropriate to call someone a son of Belial because he accidentally parked in the place where the pastor's wife usually parks.

4. In *Angels in the Architecture*, I argued that confessions and creeds are like fence posts around a garden. Systematic expressions of the faith should allow for a more organic (and "sloppy") form of biblical expression inside the fence. The high creedalists want the whole garden to be nothing but fence posts all the way across. And the poetic dreamers want to tear down the fence for the sake of biblical expression, but the only thing that happens is that all the heretical deer come in and eat everything. This is why I want us to continue to affirm an effectual-call regeneration as one of our key fence posts. This should not at all preclude detailed theological discussion within the garden about the differences between lettuce regeneration and arugula regeneration. So to speak.

5. One of the things we should have learned by this point is how to debate issues of this importance without losing all sense of proportion. One time in an online discussion of some Federal Vision issues—of which I apparently cannot get enough—I was asked about the difference between what I call the amber ales and the oatmeal stouts. There is not a monolithic Federal Vision position on everything and, not surprisingly, there are differences of emphasis throughout the movement as well as differences of substantive opinion. I identify myself as an amber ale, and I said that some of the oatmeal stouts, while historically orthodox and good Reformed men, were not what I would describe as historic evangelicals. I was asked what I meant, and I thought that I should make a fuller reply here.

    Incidentally, someone has pointed out that this metaphor of mine might be ceding too much to those on the other side of the question. But this presupposes a certain set of preferences in beer. By amber ale I do not mean

Bud Lite, and I prefer amber ales to oatmeal stouts, which might tell you something else.

It should be noted at the outset that I insist that the historic evangelical testimony is of the utmost importance. At the same time, I do not regard errors on this point as synonymous with heresy. There have been many believers who were not evangelicals but who were much finer Christians than I have thus far gotten around to being. I don't want the larger body of Christ to lose what the evangelicals have contributed, because I really do think it is really important. But "really important" in this instance does not mean that misunderstanding it is heretical.

The important thing is to *be* born again, and formulating your views about it correctly is less so (although still important). There have been nonevangelicals who exhibit the fruit of the new birth in everything they do, and evangelicals who don't miss a signpost on the Romans road and who yet don't exhibit the fruit of the new birth. One boy said he would work the vineyard and didn't, and the other said he would not go, and yet did. One of the things that will happen when God gives us reformation and revival is that a large number of evangelicals will get saved.

The *sine qua non* of evangelicalism is the absolute necessity of the new birth. Without that, there is no evangelicalism, and with it, there is new life and joy and gladness. There is also a *tradition* of evangelical bromides, which bring the *tradition* of saying that new life and joy and gladness would no doubt be a good thing were they ever to show up. Like Lady Catherine in *Pride and Prejudice*, had we ever taken up the pianoforte, we would have been a great proficient.

In *The Plan of Salvation*, B.B. Warfield identifies the evangelical position as that which testifies to the saving grace of God as an immediate transaction between God and the saved soul. God can perform this stupendous work in the human soul apart from means, and He can do it in accordance with means. But when He uses means, He is doing so with sovereign authority *over* the means. He is not bound to them, He is not tethered. He uses them as He sees fit. There are those present who are just as baptized, and just as preached to, who are not converted. Why not? Because the effectual call did not summon them. This effectual call is the center of historic Reformed evangelicalism.

Again, Ambrose Bierce's definition of ritualism: 'A Dutch Garden of God where He may walk in rectilinear freedom, keeping off the grass." We love to set down rules for God, either tying Him down to the rites and rituals, so that we might have our priestcraft mummeries kept safe, or to divorce Him from His appointed means entirely, lest baptism and the preached Word prove to be too much of a temptation to Him. Hyperevangelicals don't want to stumble God.

So just as the general Federal Vision movement admits of gradations, so does the opposition to it. Some of the evangelicals in opposition have so emphasized the immediacy of grace, hot off the griddles of Heaven, that this evangelical position has become a parody of itself. If you introduce any means at all, however nuanced and however qualified, they immediately start yelling about how great Diana of the Ephesians is.

But the Spirit of God blows where He wishes. You cannot see where He comes from, or where He is going. You cannot chain Him to the baptismal font, and you cannot tether Him to that *Ultimate Questions* booklet either. The fact that God ordinarily works through the lesser means of the preached word, and through the lesser grace of baptismal water, and so forth, does not diminish at all the effectual grace of the effectual call. In the salvation of an individual, that is the one thing needful, and that is the historic evangelical confession.